Breaking Bloodline Curses

Your Guide to Freedom from Generational Patterns, Cycles, and Curses

DR. MAXWELL SHIMBA

Published in Manhattan, New York by Shimba Publishing, LLC.

Shimba Publishing LLC

Table of Contents

Foreword

To the earnest seeker, the theological student, the weary warrior, and the child of Destiny who has picked up this treatise, I welcome you. You are about to embark on a journey into the deep things of God, into the mysteries that have been hidden from the casual reader but are now being revealed by His Spirit to those who are matured, to those who have graduated from milk to the solid food of advanced Kingdom understanding. Let it be known from the outset: this is not a book for the spiritual infant. The concepts we will explore, the scriptures we will rightly divide, require a mind made alert by the Spirit and a heart that is profoundly receptive. What you are about to receive is what I have termed, in my own walk with God, *food for the matured*.

For too long, a significant segment of the Body of Christ has operated with a truncated gospel, a redemption that speaks only to the personal, individual sins of the present moment, while remaining willfully ignorant of the vertical, historical dimensions of spiritual conflict. We have been content to preach a salvation that saves the soul but seems powerless to break the persistent, haunting cycles that plague our families—cycles of financial ruin, addictive behaviors, marital failure, and debilitating sickness. We have celebrated the God of Abraham, Isaac, and Jacob, the God who operates generationally in blessing, while in the same breath, with a staggering lack of self-awareness, we have dismissed the reality of generational curses as superstition or folk religion. This, my dear reader, is a critical failure in our hermeneutic, a blind spot in our spiritual warfare, and it is a luxury that the struggling child of God, trapped in a generational stronghold, can no longer afford.

I must be forthright: in my earlier years of ministry, I too was among the voices that declared, "There is no such thing as a generational curse for the believer!" It was a theologically convenient position, one that seemed to protect the finished work of the Cross from any perceived complication. But then I began to minister to real people with real, documented, multi-generational struggles. I encountered believers, fervent in prayer and faith, who were nonetheless besieged by the same giants that conquered their parents and grandparents. I saw the look of desperation in their eyes, a look that said, "I have done everything I know to do, yet here I am, facing the same enemy my father faced." It was in the trenches of pastoral ministry and deliverance that the Holy Spirit began to confront my academic presuppositions with undeniable spiritual reality. I was forced to humble myself and ask the difficult question: Have I, in my zeal to protect a doctrine, inadvertently disarmed the people of God from a vital weapon in their arsenal?

The journey of understanding begins where all true theology must begin: with the nature and character of God Himself. We must establish, with biblical veracity, that **God is a generational God**. This is the non-negotiable foundation. When He appeared to Moses at the burning bush, He did not identify Himself as a deity of the immediate moment. He declared, "I am the God of your father, the God of Abraham, the God of Isaac, and the God of Jacob" (Exodus 3:6). This self-revelation is profoundly intentional. It connects the present encounter with a covenant legacy that spans centuries. The promises He made to Abraham were not fully realized in Abraham's lifetime; they unfolded through Isaac, were wrestled over by Jacob, and formed the identity of the nation of Israel. God's mind thinks in terms of lineages, of bloodlines, of destinies that are fulfilled across the tapestry of multiple generations.

Now, if this is true—and scripture unequivocally affirms that it is—then we are faced with a theological imperative. We must, by the law of spiritual balance, acknowledge the corollary. If there is a generational transmission of blessing, there must exist, by the enemy's perverse imitation, a generational transmission of cursing. How can we define light if we refuse to acknowledge darkness? How can we comprehend up without down? How can we preach a generational blessing while simultaneously rejecting the concept of a generational curse? This is not dualism; this is the recognition of a stolen, inverted principle. Satan, the created being with no original creative power, is a master counterfeiter. He has studied the generational pathways that God established for blessing and has hijacked them to transmit iniquity, limitation, and destruction. He understands the legal power of a bloodline, and he exploits it mercilessly.

The biblical evidence for this is not confined to obscure, symbolic passages. It is embedded in the very fabric of the Law. Exodus 20:4-5 presents us with a sobering declaration: "You shall not make for yourself a carved image... for I the Lord your God am a jealous God, visiting the iniquity of the fathers on the children to the third and the fourth generation of those who hate me." The Hebrew word for "visiting," *paqad*, carries the weight of appointed oversight, of bringing to account. This is not the arbitrary punishment of innocent children; it is the revelation of a spiritual law—the consequences of sin, particularly covenant-breaking sins like idolatry, create a ripple effect through time, establishing a legal ground for demonic oppression in the lives of descendants. We see this principle enacted in the terrifying narrative of Achan in Joshua 7, where his sin of covetousness and theft brought corporate defeat and death not only upon himself but upon his sons, his daughters, and his livestock. The entire family unit was consumed by the consequence of the father's iniquity.

But the heart of our exploration, the mystery that will occupy a significant portion of our study, is found in the profound typology of the blood. We are introduced to this in the seminal passage of 1 John 5:7-8, which distinguishes between the three heavenly witnesses (the Father, the Word, the Holy Spirit) and the three earthly witnesses: **the Spirit, the Water, and the Blood**. A witness, in the biblical sense, is one who was present, one who can testify to what has occurred. The Spirit here speaks of the human spirit and its condition; the Water, as I have taught in other series, speaks of the soulical realm, emotions, and even demonic strongholds over regions and families. But it is the Blood that demands our focused attention.

The blood is the God-appointed reservoir of life. Leviticus 17:11 is unequivocal: "For the life of the flesh is in the blood." This is not merely biological fact; it is spiritual law. The blood in your veins is a witness. It is a living, speaking record. It is older than you are. It carries the genetic code from your father and your mother, but it also carries a spiritual testimony. It was present in your forefathers. It heard the vows they made, it was shaped by the sins they committed, and it carries the memory of the covenants they entered into, whether with God or with darkness. This is why David, under the inspiration of the Holy Spirit, could declare in Psalm 51:5, "Behold, I was brought forth in iniquity, and in sin did my mother conceive me." He was not confessing a personal act of sin in the womb; he was acknowledging by revelation the fallen spiritual state he inherited through the bloodline of Adam. He was a sinner by nature before he was a sinner by choice.

This understanding brings a terrifying and yet illuminating clarity to the confrontation between God and Cain in Genesis 4:10. After Cain murdered Abel, God does not say, "The soul of your brother is crying to me." He says, "The **voice of your brother's blood** cries out to me from the ground." The blood speaks. The blood of Abel bore witness to the violence, the injustice, and it cried out for one thing, and one thing only: **Vengeance**. This is the primary voice of the fallen, Adamic bloodline—a cry for justice, for retribution, for the wages of sin to be paid.

Now, consider the medical analogy of a hematologist. When you present with a mysterious ailment, what is the first thing a competent doctor does? He ignores your subjective description of the pain. He takes a sample of your blood. He submits that blood to analysis, and he trusts the testimony of that blood over your feelings, over your own assessment of your condition. The blood reveals what is truly happening at the foundational level of your life. In the same way, the spiritual hematology of your life reveals that many of your struggles are not originating from you. That compulsive thought, that addictive pull, that recurring failure, that mysterious ailment—it is not that you are not trying hard enough. It is that the **blood is speaking**. The blood is testifying to a familiar pattern, a stronghold that was established generations before you were born. It is saying, "This is who we are. This is what we do. No one in our line ever prospers. No one in our line ever remains faithful. This is our lot."

This is the prison of the "father's house" that God commanded Abraham to leave. You can physically leave a country, you can distance yourself from your extended family, but if you have not spiritually exited the "father's house"—the core bloodline inheritance of iniquity and limitation—you will simply recreate the same problems in a new location. You will move from Angola to Spain and still live in pain. You will leave Johannesburg for London and still be bound by the same spirit of poverty. The geography changes, but the spiritual inheritance remains intact.

But hear me, and hear me well, for this is the pivot upon which all hope turns: The blood of Jesus Christ speaks a better word. The writer of Hebrews, in a moment of breathtaking theological insight, declares in chapter 12, verse 24, that we have come "to Jesus, the mediator of a new covenant, and to the sprinkled blood that speaks a better word than the blood of Abel." Abel's blood cried, "Vengeance!" Jesus's blood, shed on the cross, cries, "Forgiveness! Peace! Reconciliation! Mercy!" The purity of Christ's blood, untainted by a human father, untainted by the sin of Adam, gives it an authority that transcends and silences the voice of the old bloodline. Your deliverance, your freedom, is not found in trying to sanctify the old blood, but in applying the superior, court-approved testimony of the blood of the Lamb over your life.

This is more than a positional truth; it is a legal reality that must be awakened to. When 2 Corinthians 5:17 declares, "Therefore, if anyone is in Christ, he is a new creation. The old has passed away; behold, the new has come," the word "behold" is a trumpet blast, a divine command to awaken to a new reality. Many believers are legally in Christ but are living as if they are still in Adam. They are like a prince who, unaware of his royal birth, continues to live as a pauper. The chains have been broken, but they have not yet shaken them from their wrists. Our journey will take us into the practical outworking of this—how to awaken to your new identity in Christ, how to use your tongue as a weapon of enforcement, how to take communion not as a mere symbol but as a covenant meal that applies the very life and testimony of Jesus to your body and spirit, and how to navigate the ministry of deliverance when spiritual attachments persist.

We will explore the critical distinctions between being possessed, having a spirit attached, and being under spiritual attack. We will discuss the God-ordained role of the covenanted deliverer, the man or woman of God anointed to stand in the gap and pray for your freedom, just as Jesus told Peter, "I have prayed for you." This is not a journey into fear, but into the glorious liberty of the children of God. It is a call to be the Abraham of your lineage—the one who breaks the chain, who exits the old father's house, and who establishes a new legacy of blessing for generations yet unborn. So, I invite you to turn the page with a hungry heart and a receptive spirit. Your life, I declare by the authority of God's Word, shall never be the same again.

Dr. Maxwell Shimba
Shimba Theological Institute

CHAPTER 1

The Reality of Spiritual Heredity

Beloved, gather close and lend not merely your ears, but your spirit. For we are about to embark upon a journey that will challenge the very contours of your faith, stretching it beyond the comfortable, linear path of personal piety and individual spiritual development into which many have been lulled. The modern Western church, in particular, has often presented the walk of faith as a singular, horizontal trajectory—a personal relationship with God that exists in a historical vacuum, disconnected from the weight of the past and the legacy of the future. But I declare to you today, with the full authority of the revealed Word of God, that this is a truncated gospel, a map that shows only the flatlands while ignoring the treacherous mountains and the deep, hidden rivers that have shaped the landscape of your life.

A more profound examination, one that dares to look with unflinching honesty at both the canon of Scripture and the testable reality of human experience, reveals a complex, often daunting, **vertical dimension**—a spiritual heredity that flows with the relentless force of a river from one generation to the next. This book posits, with scholarly conviction and pastoral urgency, that to ignore this vertical axis is to navigate the most critical battlefield of your life with a fatally incomplete map. You may know your position in Christ, you may be armed with the sword of the Spirit, but if you are unaware of the generational strongholds that have been established on the land you are trying to possess, you will find yourself fighting the same losing battles your fathers and mothers fought, wondering why your faith seems insufficient against an enemy that appears to know your moves before you make them.

The testimony is not merely anecdotal, though the cries of countless believers trapped in cycles of addiction, financial ruin, relational breakdown, and inexplicable illness provide a chorus of witness that cannot be ignored. No, our case is built upon a rigorous, exegetical excavation of the biblical text, from the Torah to the Epistles, which affirms with startling consistency the reality of **generational patterns, cycles, and curses**. This is not the stuff of charismatic speculation; it is the hard, sober truth of divine revelation, a truth that has been too often spiritualized into irrelevance or dismissed as an Old Testament relic. But I ask you, can a relic produce such persistent, tangible fruit in the lives of believers today? Can a mere metaphor bind a soul with such tenacious, multi-generational chains?

A foundational premise of this work, one which we will return to again and again as the bedrock of our understanding, is that **God Himself operates generationally**. This is His innate mode of operation. When the Almighty chose to reveal His covenant name and nature to Moses at the burning bush—the very theophany that would launch the Exodus—He did not introduce Himself as the God of the immediate moment, nor as a deity concerned only with individual transactions. No, His self-identification was profoundly, intentionally generational: "I am the God of your father, the God of Abraham, the God of Isaac, and the God of Jacob" (Exodus 3:6). In this one declaration, He connects the present crisis to a covenant legacy spanning centuries. He anchors Moses's destiny not in his own faltering abilities, but in the unbroken thread of a promise made to his forefathers. The promises He spoke over Abraham were not fully realized in Abraham's lifetime; they were carried in the loins of Isaac, wrestled over by Jacob, and forged in the crucible of Joseph's suffering. God's mind, His administrative strategy, thinks in terms of lineages, of bloodlines, of destinies that are fulfilled across the grand, unfolding tapestry of multiple generations. He is the God of the long view, the God of the legacy.

This divine principle, however, established in the very nature of God's covenant dealings, has a terrifying and powerful corollary in the realm of darkness. The kingdom of Satan is, by its very nature, a parasitic, imitative kingdom. The enemy, a created being, possesses no original creative power. His genius is one of perversion, of counterfeit, of inversion. He sees the generational pathways that God has established for the transmission of blessing, and he establishes his own infernal conduits for the transmission of death. Just as blessings, promises, and a divine mantle can be inherited, so can **iniquities, predispositions, spiritual limitations, and demonic legal rights**. The same riverbed that God designed to carry life-giving water can be poisoned at its source and used to carry a deadly toxin to everyone downstream.

Therefore, to accept the reality of generational blessing while simultaneously rejecting the possibility of generational curses is not merely an oversight; it is a profound **theological inconsistency** that what I have termed in my ministry the "law of balance" simply does not permit. You cannot have a coherent theology of light without acknowledging the reality of darkness. You cannot define "up" without its opposite, "down." How can we, with any intellectual or spiritual integrity, preach with fervor about the "God of Abraham, Isaac, and Jacob" and the blessings that flow to a thousand generations of those who love Him, while in the same breath dismissing the clear biblical teaching that He "visits the iniquity of the fathers on the children to the third and the fourth generation" (Exodus 20:5)? This is not a contradiction in God; it is a revelation of a consistent spiritual law that operates in both directions. To ignore one half of this equation is to render ourselves powerless against it. It is to stand in a warzone and declare that only friendly forces have the capacity to use the terrain to their advantage, while the enemy is somehow confined to open fields. This is a lethal delusion.

It is for this reason that this text is unapologetically crafted for "the matured," for those who are ready to move beyond the elementary principles of Christ and onto the solid food that belongs to those of full age (Hebrews 5:14, 1 Corinthians 2:6). We are dealing here with the "deep things" of the spirit, the *bathos* of God, the mysteries that are revealed not to the casual observer but to the hungry, the diligent, the one who is willing to search out a matter as for hidden treasure. We will venture into the mystery of bloodlines, not with the superstitious fear of the occultist, but with the sober confidence of the blood-bought saint who understands that Christ has provided a **complete redemption**—a redemption so comprehensive, so all-encompassing, that it addresses every facet of the fallen human condition, including those aspects we *inherit* rather than those we personally cultivate. The Cross of Calvary is not merely the antidote for your personal sins; it is the judicial instrument that severs the legal claims of ancestral sin. It is the divine axe laid to the root of the generational tree.

Our methodology, therefore, must be and will be strictly, unwaveringly biblical. We will build our case not on anecdote alone, nor on psychological theory, but on a "rightly dividing" (2 Timothy 2:15, KJV) of the Word of Truth. This Greek word, *orthotomeō*, carries the vivid imagery of cutting a straight path, of skillfully dissecting and laying open a text to reveal its true meaning and application. We will be spiritual surgeons, opening the body of Scripture to trace the arteries of generational influence. We will explore the profound implications of the three that bear witness on earth—the Spirit, the Water, and the Blood—and how their testimony creates a spiritual record that can either imprison or liberate. We will delve into the typologies of the Old Testament narratives, seeing in the lives of the patriarchs not just ancient stories of faith, but living, breathing case studies in generational patterns and their divine interruption.

The ultimate goal of this exploration is not to foster a spirit of blame, of pointing fingers at long-dead ancestors and abdicating personal responsibility. Nor is it to cultivate a victim mentality, where one is perpetually defined by the failures of the past. Absolutely not. The goal is the exact opposite: to equip the "child of Destiny" with the knowledge, the spiritual authority, and the practical tools to **break every chain**. It is to move you from a position of passive suffering to active, aggressive warfare. It is to hand you the title deed to your own life, showing you how to evict the squatters that have occupied your bloodline for generations. It is to ensure, by the power of the Holy Spirit and the authority of the name of Jesus, that "what stopped others will not stop you." That the giant that conquered your grandfather will be a decapitated corpse at your feet. That the cycle of poverty that has haunted your family for a century will end with you, and you will become a fountainhead of generational blessing for your children and your children's children. This is your inheritance. This is your destiny. And it begins with understanding the reality of the battlefield upon which you stand.

CHAPTER 02

Hermeneutical Foundations: Establishing the Biblical Case

My brothers and sisters, we now stand at the threshold of the most critical phase of our study. Before we dare to step into the practical deliverance, before we can authoritatively lay the axe to the root of these generational trees, we must first ensure that we are standing on unshakable ground. We must build, with painstaking care and exegetical precision, a sound hermeneutical foundation. The doctrine of generational iniquity and its consequences cannot, must not, rest on the shifting sands of personal experience, psychological theory, or charismatic tradition alone. If it is to bear the weight of your destiny and the fury of the enemy's counterattack, it must be anchored to the immovable bedrock of clear, contextual, and consistent biblical premises. We are not spiritual detectives inventing a crime; we are biblical theologians uncovering a long-established, divinely-revealed legal statute.

The primary scriptural cornerstone, the *locus classicus* for this entire teaching, is etched by the very finger of God into the stone of Sinai. It is found in the heart of the Decalogue, the moral law that defines the character of God and the covenant relationship with His people. Exodus 20:4-5 thunders from the mountain: "You shall not make for yourself a carved image... You shall not bow down to them or serve them; for I the Lord your God am a jealous God, **visiting the iniquity of the fathers on the children to the third and the fourth generation of those who hate me.**"

Now, we must pause here and dissect this with the scalpel of the Spirit. The English word "visiting" is a pale shadow of the rich, heavy Hebrew word *paqad* (פָּקַד). This is not a casual drop-in. *Paqad* carries the weight of divine oversight, of appointed judgment, of mustering for a specific purpose. It is the word used when God "visited" Sarah to open her womb (Genesis 21:1). It is the word used when God "attended to" the cry of the Israelites in Egypt (Exodus 4:31). It is a word of sovereign, purposeful action. This "visitation" of iniquity, therefore, is not an arbitrary, capricious outburst of divine wrath against innocent children. It is the sober, judicial revelation of a **spiritual law of consequence** that God Himself has built into the moral fabric of His creation. Just as the law of gravity ensures that a stone dropped from a tower will fall, this spiritual law ensures that unrepentant, covenant-breaking sin sets in motion a chain of consequences that reverberate through family lines.

The specific iniquity cited here is paramount: **idolatry**. This is the master sin, the root from which all other familial and societal curses ultimately spring. Idolatry is not merely the bowing to a statue; it is a fundamental transfer of trust, worship, and covenant allegiance from the One True God to a demonic counterfeit. As Paul confirms in 1 Corinthians 10:20, "I imply that what pagans sacrifice they offer to demons and not to God." When a father enters into a covenant with a demonic power through idolatry, he is not acting in a vacuum. He is, in a very real spiritual and legal sense, signing a treaty on behalf of his household. He is opening a door, establishing a beachhead for demonic influence that, unless decisively broken, will provide a familiar and welcoming environment for that same spirit to operate in his children and grandchildren. The patterns of behavior—the deceit, the sexual immorality, the love of power, the rejection of true authority—that accompany that idolatry are then passed down, not just by social learning, but by spiritual affinity.

This terrifying principle is not a one-off declaration. It is a consistent drumbeat throughout the Pentateuch, a foundational chord in God's self-revelation. In Exodus 34:6-7, in the glorious aftermath of the golden calf incident, God proclaims His compassionate, gracious, and merciful character. Yet, in the very same breath, He reaffirms the unyielding nature of His justice: "...keeping steadfast love for thousands, forgiving iniquity and transgression and sin, but **who will by no means clear the guilty, visiting the iniquity of the fathers on the children and the children's children, to the third and the fourth generation.**" Do you see the balance? His mercy is vast, extending to *thousands* of generations of those who love Him, but His justice will not simply ignore the legal claims established by sin. The "guilty" here refers to the one who commits the original, high-handed sin, but the "visitation" falls upon the lineage.

This brings us to the critical objection, the one that has caused many to stumble: the prophecy of Ezekiel 18. "The soul who sins shall die. The son shall not suffer for the iniquity of the father..." (Ezekiel 18:20). Superficially, this appears to contradict Exodus. But this is where right division is essential. Ezekiel 18 is a pastoral correction against a fatalistic folk theology in Babylonian exile, where people were blaming their fathers for their plight while continuing in the same sinful patterns themselves. God is declaring that each person is morally accountable for their *own* sins and can, through personal repentance, step out from under the *corporate consequences* of their father's sins. It deals with personal guilt and salvation. Exodus 20 and 34 deal with the **corporate consequence and legal ground** of unrepented, covenant-breaking sin. A child is not guilty of their father's idolatry, but they may suffer its tangible, spiritual consequences—the demonic oppression, the familial patterns, the brokenness—until someone in that bloodline rises up with authority and severs the legal claim through repentance and the blood of Jesus. The child may live in a house plagued by termites because of the father's poor construction; the child is not guilty of the poor construction, but they must deal with the collapsing floors until the house is repaired.

Numbers 14:18 provides the third witness, as Moses pleads for the nation after the rebellion of the spies, quoting God's own character back to Him: "The Lord is slow to anger and abounding in steadfast love, forgiving iniquity and transgression, but he will by no means clear the guilty, visiting the iniquity of the fathers on the children, to the third and the fourth generation." The consistency of this testimony across the Law of Moses establishes it beyond any doubt as a foundational spiritual law.

But the biblical case does not rest on legislative texts alone. Scripture provides us with a harrowing, narrative case study that puts flesh and blood on this skeletal legal framework: the sin of Achan in Joshua 7. After the stunning victory at Jericho, Israel suffers a humiliating defeat at the tiny outpost of Ai. The reason is covenant unfaithfulness. One man, Achan, from the tribe of Judah no less, coveted and took devoted things from Jericho, things that were *cherem*—devoted to destruction, set apart for the Lord alone. He took a beautiful cloak, silver, and gold, and hid them in the earth *inside his tent*.

When Joshua, by the Lord's direction, identifies Achan, the consequences are stark and corporate. Joshua 7:24-25 records: "And Joshua and all Israel with him took Achan the son of Zerah, and the silver and the cloak and the bar of gold, and his sons and his daughters and his oxen and his donkeys and his sheep and his tent and all that he had. And all Israel stoned him with stones... and they burned them with fire and stoned them with stones." His entire household, his livestock, and his possessions were consumed in the judgment. Why? Because Achan's sin was not a private affair. By bringing the accursed thing into his tent, he brought a curse upon his entire household. His family, his children, lived under the covering of his covenant headship. His sin of covetousness and theft opened a door to a spirit of deception and greed that, left unchecked, would have contaminated the entire nation. This narrative illustrates with terrifying clarity the corporate nature of sin and its consequences within a family unit. It reveals the power of a **generational spirit of covetousness and disobedience**, showing how the sin of the father can legally and spiritually implicate the entire household.

And finally, we look to the prophet Daniel, a man of unparalleled righteousness and divine favor, who understood this corporate, generational reality at the deepest level. Living in Babylonian exile, he did not stand aloof, pointing the finger at his sinful ancestors. Instead, in one of the most profound prayers of identification and repentance in all of Scripture, he cried out: "**We have sinned and done wrong and acted wickedly and rebelled, turning aside from your commandments and rules... O Lord, to us belongs open shame, to our kings, to our princes, and to our fathers, because we have sinned against you**" (Daniel 9:5, 8). Daniel, a righteous man, included himself in the corporate "we" of his nation's generational rebellion. He recognized that the captivity they were experiencing, the delay in the fulfillment of Jeremiah's prophecy, was the direct fruit of generations of accumulated iniquity. He did not plead his own innocence; he stood in the gap, repenting for the sins of his forefathers, acknowledging the justness of the generational consequence, and appealing to God's mercy to now relent and restore. In Daniel, we see the ultimate model: the child of Destiny who understands the vertical dimension of sin, who does not blame but identifies, who does not excuse but repents, and in doing so, becomes the very instrument God uses to break the curse and release a new season of destiny for his entire people.

...And finally, we must fix our gaze upon the prophet Daniel, for in him we find not merely a proof-text, but a living, breathing paradigm of how a righteous man, a "child of Destiny," rightly discerns and engages with the stark reality of generational iniquity. Daniel, a man of unparalleled righteousness and divine favor, a man in whom no discernible fault could be found by his most ardent enemies, a man who enjoyed direct angelic visitation and the profound revelation of the seventy weeks—

this same Daniel did not stand aloof in self-righteous isolation, pointing an accusatory finger at his sinful ancestors. He did not adopt the modern, individualistic heresy that would say, "I am not responsible for the sins of my fathers." No! He understood the corporate, spiritual-solidarity reality of the covenant at the deepest level of his spirit.

Living in the humiliation of the Babylonian exile, with the promised land a distant memory and the temple lies in ruins, Daniel did not attribute their plight to bad geopolitical luck or the superior military strategy of Nebuchadnezzar. He possessed prophetic sight. He saw through the veil of natural circumstances and perceived the true, spiritual root of their national catastrophe. And so, in one of the most profound, gut-wrenching prayers of identification and repentance in all of Scripture, he tore open his soul and cried out:

"We have sinned and done wrong and acted wickedly and rebelled, turning aside from your commandments and rules... O Lord, to us belongs open shame, to our kings, to our princes, and to our fathers, because we have sinned against you. To the Lord our God belong mercy and forgiveness, for we have rebelled against him and have not obeyed the voice of the LORD our God by walking in his laws, which he set before us by his servants the prophets. All Israel has transgressed your law and turned aside, refusing to obey your voice. And the curse and oath that are written in the Law of Moses the servant of God have been poured out upon us, because we have sinned against him." (Daniel 9:5-6, 9-11)

Do you hear the pronouns? Do you feel the weight of his identification? "**We** have sinned." "To **us** belongs open shame."

"**All Israel** has transgressed." This is not the language of personal guilt alone; this is the language of **corporate responsibility and generational identification**. Daniel, a righteous man, included himself in the corporate "we" of his nation's multi-generational rebellion. He recognized with stunning clarity that the captivity they were experiencing, the delay in the fulfillment of Jeremiah's prophecy of restoration, was the direct, tangible fruit of generations of accumulated, unrepented iniquity. The "curse... written in the Law of Moses" was not a theoretical concept; it was their present, bitter reality. He understood that the consequences of the fathers' sins—the idolatry of Manasseh, the rebellion of the kings, the apostasy of the priests—had created a spiritual debt, a legal ground, that held the entire nation in bondage.

He did not plead his own innocence. He did not say, "But Lord, I was faithful in the lion's den! I was faithful with the king's food!" Instead, he stood in the gap, as a priest of his people, and repented *for the sins of his forefathers*. He acknowledged the justness of the generational consequence, and in that place of profound humility and identification, he appealed to God's covenant mercy and His own righteous reputation to now relent and restore. He prayed, **"O Lord, according to all your righteous acts, let your anger and your wrath turn away from your city Jerusalem... O my God, incline your ear and hear. Open your eyes and see our desolations, and the city that is called by your name. For we do not present our pleas before you because of our righteousness, but because of your great mercy."** (Daniel 9:16, 18).

In Daniel, we see the ultimate model for our ministry today. He is the prototype of the awakened "child of Destiny" who understands the vertical dimension of sin. He is the one who does not blame his ancestors but identifies with the corporate brokenness. He does not excuse the sin but courageously repents for it, even when it is not personally his own. He does not deny the curse but brings it into the light before a merciful God. And in doing so, he becomes the very instrument, the chosen vessel, through whom God breaks the power of the generational curse, interprets the times, and releases a new season of destiny, restoration, and prophetic fulfillment for his entire people. His prayer was the key that unlocked the heavens and initiated the process of return from exile. Your prayer, your informed, identificational repentance, can be the key that unlocks your family from its generational exile.

Therefore, the biblical case for generational influences is robust, multi-faceted, and utterly undeniable. It is not a peripheral doctrine found in a few obscure verses; it is a principle woven into the very fabric of God's dealings with humanity, from the Law to the Prophets to the Wisdom literature. It reveals a fundamental truth about our existence: that **no man is an island**. We are not self-created atoms bouncing in a void. Each one of us is a link in a chain—a chain that stretches backward through time, carrying the weight of our forebears' choices, and forward into the future, carrying the legacy we ourselves are now forging. To pretend otherwise is not piety; it is profound ignorance. It is to deny the clear testimony of Scripture and the consistent witness of human experience. We are born into a spiritual ecosystem, an environment shaped by the sins and the faithfulness of those who came before us. And while we bear the image of God and possess a will of our own, we do not exercise that will on a blank slate. We fight our battles on a battlefield that has been pre-shaped by the victories and defeats of our lineage. To ignore the topography of this battlefield, to refuse to study the strategies of the enemy that have been successful against your bloodline in the past, is not faith—it is folly. It is to walk blindly into an ambush that has been successfully sprung on your family for generations.

This is why the ministry of John the Baptist, the forerunner of Christ, was prophesied in the language of generational healing: **"And he will go on before the Lord, in the spirit and power of Elijah, to turn the hearts of the parents to their children and the disobedient to the wisdom of the righteous—to make ready a people prepared for the Lord."** (Luke 1:17). The "spirit and power of Elijah" is, in part, the anointing to deal with fractured generational lines, to heal the breaches between fathers and children that have allowed curses to flourish. It is the ministry of restoration that prepares the way for the Lord Himself to come and establish a new covenant—a covenant that, as we shall see, provides the ultimate and final answer to this entire devastating problem. But you cannot apply the cure until you have accurately diagnosed the disease. You cannot claim the victory of the New Covenant over generational curses if you refuse to believe that such curses exist or have any legitimate power. The blood of Jesus is the antidote to a real poison. To deny the poison is to nullify your need for the antidote, leaving you to suffer its effects while boasting of your immunity.

CHAPTER 03

The Triune Witness on Earth: Spirit, Water, and Blood

Beloved, we have now laid the unshakable legal foundation from the Law and the Prophets. We have established beyond any righteous doubt that generational iniquity is not a theological fiction but a devastating spiritual reality. But a critical question now demands an answer: *How?* By what mechanism is this spiritual poison transmitted? How does the failure of a great-grandfather, a sin committed decades or even centuries ago, reach across the chasm of time to manifest as a compulsive behavior, a mysterious illness, or a spirit of failure in your life today? To answer this, we must be initiated into one of the most profound mysteries of the faith—the mystery of the **Triune Witness on Earth**.

To comprehend this, you must first grasp the biblical concept of a "witness." In the divine court of heaven, a witness is not a passive observer. A witness is a legal entity that was present at an event and can therefore provide authoritative, court-admissible testimony about it. In the mouth of two or three witnesses, a matter is established (Deuteronomy 19:15). This concept is masterfully and precisely presented in the first epistle of John, chapter 5, verses 7 and 8. The King James Version renders it with majestic clarity:

"For there are three that bear record in heaven, the Father, the Word, and the Holy Ghost: and these three are one. And there are three that bear witness in earth, the Spirit, and the water, and the blood: and these three agree in one."

While the three heavenly witnesses—the Father, the Word (the Lord Jesus Christ), and the Holy Ghost—testify to the nature and unity of the Godhead, the three earthly witnesses testify to the reality of life on this planet. They are the divine instruments of record-keeping for the human experience. When the Righteous Judge of all the earth seeks to understand what has transpired in a human life, in a family line, or in a nation, He consults these three witnesses. They are the immutable ledger. They "agree in one"; their testimony is seamless, consistent, and utterly undeniable. They form a complete picture, and it is through their combined testimony that spiritual realities, including generational iniquities, are given legal standing and transmitted.

Today, we will delve into the first of these earth-shaking witnesses. We will pull back the veil on **The Spirit**.

Now, we must proceed with precision. The "Spirit" mentioned in verse 8 as an earthly witness is distinct from the "Holy Ghost" mentioned in verse 7 as a heavenly witness. The context makes this undeniable. The Holy Spirit is God; He is a heavenly witness to the Son. The spirit here, in the earthly triad, is speaking of the **human spirit**. Proverbs 20:27 declares, "The spirit of man is the lamp of the LORD, searching all his innermost parts." Your spirit is the foundational core of your being, the eternal part of you that was created to be the dwelling place of God. It is the candle of the Lord, designed to be illuminated by the Holy Spirit, bringing light and divine intelligence to your soul and body.

But this human spirit, this lamp, is also a **recorder**. It is a living, spiritual hard drive that captures and stores the data of your existence. It carries the indelible record of your experiences, your choices, your deepest decisions, and the fundamental quality of your relationship with God. It is the seat of your conscience, your intuition, and your capacity for communion with the Divine. When you are born again, your spirit is instantly regenerated, made new, and sealed by the Holy Spirit (2 Corinthians 5:17, Ephesians 1:13). It becomes a new creation, a clean slate in its fundamental nature.

However—and this is a mystery of profound importance—the human spirit, while made new in its *nature*, can still be a repository of *records* and *influences* from the past. It exists within a matrix, a spiritual lineage. Just as a newborn baby, though a new soul, inherits a biological and genetic legacy from its parents, so too does the human spirit enter this world connected to a spiritual legacy. This is the terrifying reality of what we might call **ancestral spiritual conditions**.

Your human spirit can be, and often is, shaped and influenced by the spiritual environment of your bloodline before you even draw your first breath. It is like a radio receiver, pre-tuned to certain frequencies. If your father and grandfather walked in a spirit of fear, your spirit—your receiver—may come into this world with a heightened sensitivity to the frequency of fear. It does not mean you are possessed by a spirit of fear, but it means the antenna of your spirit has been bent towards that signal, making you more susceptible to its broadcast, more likely to interpret the static of life through the filter of anxiety. If your lineage was marked by a spirit of divination or occult involvement, your spirit may carry a record of that illegal covenant, an openness to supernatural revelation that does not originate from the Holy Spirit. This is why certain families have a "knack" for the psychic, the intuitive, the manipulative—it is a perverted spiritual gift, a familial anointing for the demonic.

This shaping is not merely passive. Your human spirit is in constant communion with the spiritual realm, both the kingdom of light and the kingdom of darkness. The choices of your ancestors created legal rights for demonic spirits to operate in and around your bloodline. These spirits, these familiar spirits, know the "tune" of your family line. They know the weaknesses, the iniquities, the cracks in the foundation. And they broadcast their lies, their temptations, their accusations, directly toward the human spirit, seeking to trigger the old, pre-programmed responses. They speak to the *record* in the spirit, trying to get you to play the same old song that your fathers played.

When a person feels a compulsive pull toward a sin that they genuinely hate, when they find themselves repeating a destructive pattern despite their best intentions and fervent prayers, it is often because the enemy is successfully speaking to an unhealed, unrenounced *record* in the human spirit—a record that was inscribed there by generational iniquity. The spirit, though redeemed, is still receiving data based on the old, corrupted "settings." The spirit of a man may be willing, but the flesh is weak because the flesh is being empowered by a demonic force that has legal access through an unreckoned-with ancestral record.

This is why the renewal of the mind (Romans 12:2) is not a passive process. It is an active, aggressive campaign of re-programming. It is the process by which the redeemed human spirit, now indwelt by the Holy Spirit, begins to overwrite the old, demonic records with the truth of the Word of God. It is the Holy Spirit bearing witness with *our* spirit that we are children of God (Romans 8:16), shouting down the lying testimonies of the past. When you declare, "I am the righteousness of God in Christ Jesus," you are not just making a positive confession. You are issuing a legal decree from the court of heaven, you are writing a new entry into the ledger of your human spirit, you are re-tuning the receiver to the frequency of Zion. You are commanding your spirit to agree with the testimony of heaven over the echo of the generational curse.

The human spirit, therefore, is the primary battlefield. It is the first witness. It testifies to *how* something happened. It bears witness to the spiritual posture, the inner decisions, the covenants made, the wounds received, and the allegiances formed by your ancestors. It carries the record of their relationship with God—whether one of faith and obedience or rebellion and idolatry. And that record becomes a landscape, a terrain, upon which the battles of your life are fought. To ignore this witness is to ignore the very ground you are standing on. But to understand it, to bring the light of Christ to its hidden records, is to disarm the enemy at the most fundamental level and to reclaim the territory of your destiny for the Kingdom of God.

We have now encountered the first and most intimate of the earthly witnesses—the human spirit, the lamp of the Lord, the recorder of our deepest choices and the inheritor of ancestral spiritual conditions. But the testimony does not stand on one witness alone. The divine court requires a second voice to establish the matter, and this brings us to the profound and often misunderstood second witness: **The Water**.

Throughout the canon of Scripture, water is a symbol of immense depth and fluidity, carrying a duality of meaning that reflects its very nature—it can be a source of life or a vehicle of death. On one hand, water represents the cleansing, life-giving **Word of God**. Ephesians 5:26 speaks of Christ sanctifying the church "by the washing of water with the word." It is the agent of spiritual purification and refreshment, as in the Psalmist's cry, "As the deer pants for flowing streams, so pants my soul for you, O God" (Psalm 42:1).

Yet, water simultaneously symbolizes the tumultuous, unstable realm of the **soul and the masses of humanity**. In Revelation 17:15, the angel explicitly interprets the vision for John: "The waters that you saw, where the prostitute is seated, are peoples and multitudes and nations and languages." Here, water is not cleansing; it is the chaotic, collective sea of humanity, the realm of shifting opinions, cultural currents, and soulish emotions. It is the domain of the "soul life," the Greek *psuche*, which encompasses the mind, will, and emotions—the seat of human personality and identity apart from the spirit.

In a generational context, this second witness—the Water—represents the **collective "soul life" of a family lineage**. It is the powerful, unseen current that carries the traditions, the emotional patterns, the unconscious beliefs, the unspoken rules, and the cultural strongholds from one generation to the next. If the human spirit is the internal, individual recorder, the Water is the external, communal river in which that spirit is immersed from birth.

Consider the dynamics of a family. A child is born not only with a spirit pre-tuned to certain frequencies, as we discussed, but is immediately plunged into the "water" of its family's soul life. It learns what to fear without being told. It absorbs beliefs about money, relationships, authority, and God that are never formally taught but are communicated through a thousand subtle cues, tones of voice, emotional reactions, and family narratives. A grandfather's bitterness over a business failure becomes a family-wide spirit of distrust and risk-aversion. A grandmother's grief becomes a generational melody of melancholy. A father's rejection creates a tidal wave of performance-based acceptance that shapes his children and his children's children. These are not merely psychological phenomena; they are spiritual currents. They are the "water" in which the fish swims, so ever-present that it is never questioned, only absorbed.

This is where the teachings on **"water spirits"** become critically important. In the spiritual realm, there are demonic entities that specialize in operating through this soulish, emotional, collective dimension. They are spirits that rule over the "waters" of families, communities, and even nations. They are the "principalities and powers" (Ephesians 6:12) that exploit these generational soul-currents. A "water spirit" is not necessarily a spirit that literally dwells in physical H_2O, though they can manifest near bodies of water as seen in the Gadarene demoniac who lived among the tombs *by the sea* (Mark 5:1-13). Rather, they are spirits that operate in the *soulish realm*—the realm of emotions, trauma, collective thinking, and familial traditions.

These spirits work to pollute the "water" of a family line. They stir up and feed on emotional strongholds:

- A spirit of *Rejection* will work to ensure that the emotional pattern of abandonment and isolation is passed down, perhaps through an absentee father in one generation and a critical, emotionally distant mother in the next.
- A spirit of *Poverty* will not just attack finances; it will shape a *poverty mindset*—a soul-level belief in scarcity, a fear of generosity, and a identity of lack that becomes a self-fulfilling prophecy.
- A spirit of *Heaviness* (Isaiah 61:3) will attach itself to a family's grief, turning a season of mourning into a multi-generational inheritance of depression and hopelessness.

These spirits are "familiar spirits" (Leviticus 20:27) in the truest sense of the word—they are *familiar* with the family. They know the "song" of that bloodline's soul. They know which emotional chords to strike to produce the same discordant symphony generation after generation. They work through the "water"—the soulish environment—to influence the human spirit and manipulate the physical body.

The testimony of the Water, therefore, is the testimony of the *emotional and soulish environment*. It answers the question: *In what context did these events happen?* It bears witness to the atmosphere of fear, the culture of shame, the tradition of idolatry, or the legacy of betrayal that has shaped the family. When the Water and the Spirit agree in their testimony—when the internal record of the human spirit (e.g., a predisposition to fear) aligns with the external, soulish environment (e.g., a family tradition of anxiety)—a powerful and persistent generational stronghold is established. The demonic legal right is reinforced, and the pattern becomes deeply entrenched.

Breaking the power of this witness requires more than just personal deliverance for an individual; it requires a cleansing of the "water." This is the ministry of the Word of God. Just as Jesus calmed the stormy sea with a word (Mark 4:39), the spoken, authoritative Word of God can rebuke and calm the troubled "waters" of a family's soul life. It involves a deliberate rejection of soulish traditions that contradict the truth of God (Colossians 2:8). It requires the intentional creation of new, godly family cultures—new "waters" of grace, faith, and love—into which the next generation can be immersed. It is the process of being transformed by the renewing of your *mind* (Romans 12:2), which is the primary faculty of the soul, thereby changing the very quality of the "water" in your lineage.

The witness of the Water is powerful, for it is the medium of our earliest and most profound shaping. But praise be to God, the blood of Jesus and the washing of the water of the Word provide a cleansing flood that can purify any contamination, calm any storm, and redefine the very spiritual ecosystem of your bloodline for generations to come.

We arrive now at the climax of this terrestrial triad, the most tangible, the most potent, and the most sobering of the three earthly witnesses: **The Blood**. If the Spirit is the internal recorder and the Water is the external current, then the Blood is the very river of life itself, the sacred scroll upon which the history of a lineage is indelibly written. We tread here on holy ground, for we are speaking of the very substance that God Himself has designated as the seat of life and the central agent of both condemnation and redemption.

The divine statute is proclaimed in Leviticus 17:11 with absolute, non-negotiable clarity: **"For the life of the flesh is in the blood."** This is not a primitive, pre-scientific observation. This is a divine decree that establishes a permanent spiritual law. The blood is not merely a biological fluid that transports oxygen and nutrients. In the economy of God, it is the God-appointed reservoir and conduit of *nephesh*—the life, the soul, the very animating force of a living creature. It is, therefore, sacred. It is set apart. It is the physical manifestation of a spiritual reality.

Because the blood carries the *life*, it carries the *record* of that life. From a biological perspective, this is undeniable. Your blood carries your DNA—the intricate genetic code that determines your physical form, your predispositions to certain diseases, the color of your eyes, and the shape of your hands. This genetic information is not your own invention; it is an inheritance. It is a biological testimony passed down from your parents, and from their parents, stretching back through countless generations. The blood in your veins is, biologically speaking, older than you are. It is a living library containing the records of your ancestors.

But hear me, and hear me well, for we must press into the deeper revelation: if this is true in the natural, how much more true is it in the spiritual? From a spiritual perspective, the blood also carries a record. It is a witness. It was *present* in your forefathers. It coursed through the veins of your grandfather when he made that fateful vow. It was in your mother's body when she endured that traumatic wound. It was in your father's heart when he bowed his knee to an idol. The blood is a living witness to every covenant made, every sin committed, every word spoken in authority, and every trauma endured by your lineage. It is the unbroken stream of physical and spiritual heredity.

This is why the voice of blood is so powerful in Scripture. We saw it in Genesis 4:10, where God declares to Cain, **"The voice of your brother's blood cries out to me from the ground."** Abel's blood was not silent. It was a witness. It testified to the violence, the injustice, the murder. And its cry was one of vengeance, of a demand for justice according to the law of retribution. This is the primary voice of the fallen, Adamic bloodline—a cry for the wages of sin to be paid. It speaks of guilt, of consequence, of a legal claim that has not been satisfied.

This understanding brings terrifying clarity to the patterns we see. When a spirit of the same sickness—be it cancer, heart disease, or diabetes—manifests generationally, it is not a mere coincidence of genetics. It is the blood bearing witness to a weakness, a breach in the wall, a legal ground that a demonic spirit of infirmity knows how to exploit. When a pattern of the same sin—a spirit of lust, of deception, of violence—recurs in a family, it is the blood speaking, recalling a familiar path, testifying to an ancient stronghold that has never been torn down. The blood says, "This is our story. This is what happens to us. This is who we are." It is the tangible, life-level testimony of *what happened*.

Consider the profound medical analogy of the hematologist. When you present with a mysterious ailment, the doctor does not trust your subjective description of the pain. He goes directly to the witness. He takes a sample of your *blood*. He submits that blood to analysis, and he trusts its testimony over your feelings. The blood reveals the hidden truth: a lurking infection, a chemical imbalance, a genetic marker for disease. It tells the story of what is happening at the most foundational level of your physical life. In the same way, God, the Divine Hematologist, looks to the blood as a witness to the spiritual condition of a life, of a family line. It testifies to the realities that the soul may be in denial about and that the spirit may be oppressed by.

This triad—Spirit, Water, and Blood—now forms a complete and devastatingly coherent testimony before the court of heaven.

- The **Spirit** (the human spirit) testifies to *how* something happened. It bears witness to the internal, spiritual posture—the pride, the unbelief, the idolatry, the faith, or the obedience. It is the record of the *why* behind the action.
- The **Water** (the soul life) testifies to the *context* in which it happened. It bears witness to the emotional environment, the familial traditions, the cultural strongholds, the unspoken beliefs that shaped the decision. It is the record of the *atmosphere*.
- The **Blood** testifies to *what* happened. It bears witness to the tangible, historical events—the specific sins, the covenants, the traumas, the biological imprints. It is the record of the *action* and its *physical consequences*.

When a pattern of sin, sickness, or failure persists through a family line, these three witnesses are in perfect, horrifying agreement. The Spirit testifies to a generational spiritual weakness (e.g., a predisposition to fear). The Water testifies to a generational soulish environment that reinforces it (e.g., a family culture of anxiety and control). And the Blood testifies to the generational physical manifestation (e.g., a history of stress-induced heart disease). Their combined testimony is seamless, consistent, and legally airtight in the realm of spiritual authority. They perpetuate a consistent story from one generation to the next, creating a demonic legal right that empowers familiar spirits to continue their destructive work.

Therefore, any biblically sound ministry of deliverance, any genuine attempt to break a generational curse, **must address all three witnesses**. To cast out a demon without addressing the record in the human spirit is to invite re-infestation. To renounce a sin without cleansing the soulish "water" of the family culture is to leave the toxic environment intact. To pray for healing without breaking the curse carried in the bloodline is to treat a symptom while the disease rages on.

The blood, as the carrier of life itself, as the most tangible and powerful witness, demands our particular and focused attention. How can this voice, crying for vengeance, be silenced? How can this ancient record, this scroll of condemnation, be erased? The answer to this paramount question lies at the very heart of the gospel, and it will be the sole focus of our next chapter. For the blood of Jesus Christ, the untainted, sinless Lamb of God, speaks a better word than the blood of Abel, and it is this better word that has the power to silence every accusing voice from your past and redeem the very river of life that flows through your veins.

CHAPTER 04

The Voice of the Blood: Hematology in Biblical Theology

Beloved, we now enter the holy of holies of our study, the very inner chamber where the mystery of generational transmission is both revealed and resolved. We have established that the blood is a witness. But we must now press in to understand the *content* of its testimony. We are moving from the *fact* of its voice to the *nature* of its cry. This is not a subject for the faint of heart, for it will force us to stare into the depth of our own inheritance and then, gloriously, into the fathomless depths of our redemption. We are embarking on a study of **Spiritual Hematology**—the theology of the blood.

The concept that blood has a "voice" is not, I must emphasize, a poetic metaphor, a charismatic abstraction, or a piece of mystical speculation. It is a stark, sober, and literal **biblical reality**. The Scriptures treat the blood as a conscious witness, an active testifier in the divine court. We find its genesis, its first terrible utterance, in the primal history of Genesis. After Cain murders his brother Abel, God Himself confronts the first murderer with a question that has echoed through the ages: **"What hast thou done? the voice of thy brother's blood crieth unto me from the ground."** (Genesis 4:10, KJV).

Please, pay meticulous attention to the divine language. God does not say, "The soul of your brother cries out to me from Sheol." He does not say, "The memory of this injustice is before me." He specifically, intentionally, and terrifyingly identifies the **voice of the blood**. The blood, spilled in an act of violent, jealous, premeditated murder, bore witness to the injustice. And what was the content of its cry? The context reveals it: a cry for **justice**, for **vengeance**, for the lawful penalty of life for life to be executed. The blood of Abel, the first human to die, established the foundational principle for all fallen humanity: **the blood of the Adamic line cries out for judgment.** It is a witness that accuses. It is a voice that demands retribution according to the strict letter of the law.

This voice is not a silent, inert record. It is active and potent. As the Apostle Paul affirms in 1 Corinthians 14:10, **"There are, it may be, so many kinds of voices in the world, and none of them is without signification."** The Greek word here for "signification" is *aphonos*—without meaning, without purpose, without a message. Paul's point is that every sound in creation, whether we understand its language or not, carries intelligence. The chirp of a bird, the roar of a lion, the rustle of leaves—all are forms of communication. How much more so the voice of blood, the very substance God appointed to carry life? Its voice is laden with meaning, with significance, with a specific, intelligible message in the spiritual realm.

Allow me to expand this with a powerful natural analogy, one I have developed in my own studies as **Spiritual Hematology**. Consider the medical practice of a hematologist. When you, a patient, present with a mysterious, debilitating condition, what is the first and most crucial action a competent doctor takes? He does not ultimately trust your subjective description of the pain. He does not rely solely on your perception of your own body. No. He goes directly to the primary witness. He takes a **sample of your blood**.

That vial of blood is then submitted to a battery of tests. Under the microscope, through chemical analysis, that blood begins to *testify*. It reveals hidden infections, hormonal imbalances, genetic markers for disease, and nutritional deficiencies that you, the patient, were completely unaware of. The doctor, acting as a judge in a court of medicine, then renders a diagnosis based not on your feelings, but on the **objective testimony of the blood**. He trusts the witness of the blood over the subjective experience of the patient. If the blood test reveals leukemia, it does not matter if you *feel* healthy; the court rules based on the evidence. If the blood test shows a clean bill of health, it can override your feelings of sickness. The blood is the ultimate earthly witness to the condition of the life within the flesh.

Now, transpose this entire paradigm into the spiritual realm, and the picture becomes terrifyingly clear. You may *feel* that you are struggling with a personal failure, a private sin, a unique sickness. You may berate yourself for a lack of faith or willpower. But the Divine Hematologist looks past your subjective self-assessment. He consults the witness. He looks at the **blood**. And the blood in your veins, that ancient stream inherited from your forefathers, is testifying. It is speaking a message shaped by generations of choices, covenants, and curses.

- If there is a history of idolatry in your lineage, the blood is testifying to a broken covenant with God and an illegal covenant with darkness, crying out for the judgment due to idolaters.
- If there is a history of addiction, the blood is testifying to a spirit of slavery and a curse of dependency, crying out for the consequences of that bondage.
- If there is a history of a specific illness, the blood is testifying to a genetic and spiritual vulnerability, a legal ground for a spirit of infirmity to operate.

This is why willpower and positive confession are often insufficient to break these deep strongholds. You are trying to argue with your feelings while the prosecution—the enemy of your soul—is presenting the blood as Exhibit A in the court of heaven, citing the precedent of Exodus 20:5 and the unbroken testimony of your bloodline. He is declaring, "The blood cries out! Judgment is due! This is who they are! This is their inheritance!" And based on the legal framework of the Old Covenant, his case is strong. The voice of your brother's blood, the voice of your father's blood, the voice of your own Adamic blood, is crying out against you from the ground of your generational past. This is the power, the awful, condemning power, of the first blood.

Beloved, if the natural analogy of the hematologist brings clarity, then the spiritual reality it points to operates with a precision and power that is absolute. The blood you carry in your veins is not merely a biological artifact; it is a living, spiritual transcript, a witness to the entire narrative of your ancestral line. It testifies not only to the blessings and the godly covenants your forefathers may have walked in, but with equal and often devastating force, it testifies to their sins, their iniquities, their unhealed soul wounds, and their illegal covenants with what Isaiah called "covenants with death, and with hell." (Isaiah 28:15, KJV). This is not a minor point; it is the very mechanism of the curse.

If there is a history of heart disease in your lineage, that blood testifies to more than a physical vulnerability; it bears witness to a spirit of heartache, of broken emotional covenants, of carrying burdens that were never meant to be borne, creating a legal ground for a spirit of infirmity to target that very organ. If there is a history of addiction, that blood testifies to a spiritual predisposition—a vacuum in the soul, a legacy of seeking solace in a created thing rather than the Creator, a doorway for a spirit of slavery to alcohol, to lust, to gambling, to work. The blood does not merely carry DNA; it carries a **spiritual record**, a ledger of debts and covenants that cries out for resolution.

This divine hematology explains the most perplexing and heartbreaking behaviors in believers who are genuinely, fervently born again in their spirit. A man, filled with the Holy Spirit, deeply in love with his wife, and committed to fidelity in his mind and renewed spirit, may find himself compulsively drawn into fornication, hating himself even as he moves toward the act. A woman, a tither, a prayer warrior, who deeply desires financial freedom and understands biblical principles of stewardship, may find herself perpetually haunted by debt, as if an invisible hand empties her bank account no matter how much she earns. In these agonizing struggles, the individual is often not the primary, originating source of the problem. They are fighting a ghost, a phantom limb of the soul. The **blood is speaking**. It is recalling a familiar pattern, replaying a deeply ingrained ancestral path. The blood is whispering, sometimes screaming, the old family narrative: "This is who we are. This is what we do. No one in our line has ever remained faithful. No one in our family has ever achieved lasting financial success. This is our lot. This is our story. Resistance is futile."

This is precisely why the genealogy of our Lord and Savior Jesus Christ was not a mere formality or a piece of historical trivia. It was a matter of cosmic, redemptive necessity. He could not—He absolutely *could not*—be born of the blood of Joseph, for that blood, like all human blood, carried the sin of Adam, the record of the fall, the cry for vengeance that began with Abel. The taint was in the bloodline itself. This is the profound mystery and the non-negotiable miracle of the Virgin Birth. He was conceived *not* by the will of man, nor by the blood of man, but by the overshadowing power of the Holy Spirit in the womb of the Virgin Mary (Luke 1:35). The blood that coursed through the veins of the incarnate God was pure, untainted, uncreated, divine blood. It was a new river of life sprung forth in the desert of humanity. His blood was not a witness to Adam's fall, to David's adultery, to Jacob's deception, or to the idolatry of the kings. His blood was a witness solely to the righteousness of God the Father. It had no voice of its own condemnation; its only voice was the perfect expression of the Father's will.

And this, my brothers and sisters, brings us to the glorious, earth-shattering, chain-breaking pivot of all human history and of your personal destiny. The voice of your ancestral blood is powerful, but I declare to you today, with all the authority of Heaven's court, **it is not the final authority for the believer.** The writer of Hebrews, under the divine unction of the Holy Spirit, presents the glorious, eternal contrast that is your salvation:

"You have come... to Jesus, the mediator of a new covenant, and to the sprinkled blood that speaks a better word than the blood of Abel." (Hebrews 12:24, NIV)

Let this verse break over your spirit like a tidal wave of glory. Two bloods. Two testimonies. Two covenants. Abel's blood, the blood of a fallen son of Adam, cried from the ground, from below: **"Vengeance! Justice! Judgment! Retribution!"** It was a cry *against* humanity, a cry that empowered the accuser of the brethren.

But the blood of Jesus! Oh, the blood of Jesus! It was not shed onto the ground, but was presented in the heavenly Holy of Holies, on the mercy seat of God (Hebrews 9:12). And what is its cry? It speaks a **"better word."** The Greek word is *kreitton*—stronger, more excellent, more dominant. Its voice drowns out every other voice. What does it cry? It cries, **"Forgiveness! Peace! Mercy! Reconciliation! Access! Grace!"**

The core of your deliverance from every generational curse, every haunting pattern, every accusing voice from your past, lies in this one supreme legal transaction: **silencing the testimony of the old, Adamic blood by applying the superior, court-overruling testimony of the blood of Christ.** When the enemy stands before God and plays the recording of your father's sin, of your grandfather's failure, of the bloodline's cry for judgment, you do not plead your own innocence. You point to the Cross. You present the blood of Jesus. You declare, "I appeal to a higher court! I present a better witness! The blood of Jesus speaks a better word! That old testimony is null and void! The case is dismissed! The curse is broken!" The blood of Christ does not ask for mercy; it *is* mercy. It does not beg for justice;

it *satisfied* justice. It is the final, eternal, and only word on your life and your lineage.

CHAPTER 05

Defining the Phenomena: Patterns, Curses, and Cycles

Beloved, we now stand at a critical juncture in our journey. Having established the legal and theological framework for generational transmission through the threefold witness, we must now become precise spiritual diagnosticians. In any field of serious scholarly inquiry—whether medicine, law, or theology—a precise taxonomy is not merely academic; it is the difference between a cure and a malpractice, between a just verdict and a tragic miscarriage of justice. In the realm of generational spiritual heredity, this precision is paramount. We must carefully, prayerfully, and scripturally distinguish between the related but distinct phenomena of **patterns, curses, and cycles**. A misdiagnosis here will lead to ineffective, frustrating, and ultimately failed ministry. You cannot break a curse with the prayer for a pattern, and you cannot disrupt a cycle by only addressing a curse. We must have the mind of Christ to rightly judge these spiritual realities.

Let us begin, then, with the first and most commonly observed phenomenon: **Generational Patterns**.

A generational pattern can be defined as a recognizable series of negative occurrences, behaviors, relationships, or outcomes that manifest across multiple generations within a particular family line. It is crucial to state at the outset that these patterns can be either positive—what we would call divine generational blessings—or negative, which are demonic in their origin and operation. Our focus in this treatise is, of course, on the latter, the strongholds that must be torn down.

It is vital to understand that a pattern is not necessarily a *curse* in the technical, judicial sense of a divine sentence pronounced in response to a specific, high-handed sin. A pattern can be more subtle, more ingrained in the very fabric of the family's soul life. It can be a **learned behavior** passed down through social observation and conditioning. A child who watches a parent respond to stress with rage has learned a pattern. It can be an **inherited weakness**, a vulnerability in the soul or even the body that the enemy knows how to press upon. But most significantly for our spiritual warfare, a pattern is often the playground of a **familiar spirit**—a demonic entity that knows the "playbook" of a family and knows how to exploit a recurring, unhealed point of entry to produce the same tragic outcome generation after generation.

The manifestation of a pattern is often marked by a shape-shifting quality. The core spirit remains the same, but its outward expression may adapt to the culture, personality, or opportunities of each generation. Let us take the example of a **spirit of Addiction**. A grandfather, living in an agrarian society, might have been a raging alcoholic, drowning his sorrows in homemade liquor. His son, moving to the city, becomes a workaholic, addicted to the adrenaline of success and the neglect of his family, a "respectable" addiction but just as destructive to the soul. His grandson, in the modern digital age, becomes addicted to online gambling or pornography, a hidden, private slavery. The *substance* or *behavior* changes—from alcohol to work to pixels on a screen—but the *root spirit* is the same: a spirit of Addiction, of seeking fulfillment and escape in a created thing rather than in the Creator. It is the same wolf wearing different sheep's clothing in different seasons.

We see other common patterns. The **"Firstborn Curse" or Pattern**, where firstborn children across generations face unique and similar challenges—a spirit of rejection, excessive burden, rebellion, or even premature death. We see patterns of **Marital Strife**, where divorce, infidelity, or profound emotional distance become a seemingly inevitable inheritance. We see patterns of **Business Failure or Financial Collapse**, where businesses mysteriously fail at the same point of growth, or where sudden, inexplicable debt appears just as financial breakthrough seems assured. We see patterns of **Specific Illness**, where the same type of disease—whether cancer, heart conditions, or mental illness—manifests repeatedly, suggesting not just a genetic predisposition but a spiritual legal ground for a specific spirit of infirmity.

The Biblical text provides us with a masterful and sobering case study of a deeply entrenched generational pattern: **The Pattern of Deception in the Patriarchal Line**.

It begins with the father of faith himself, **Abraham**. In Genesis 12:10-20, facing a famine, he goes down to Egypt. Fearing for his life because of his wife Sarah's beauty, he instructs her, "Say you are my sister, so that it may go well with me because of you, and that my life may be spared for your sake." This was a half-truth, a deceptive scheme born out of fear and a lack of trust in God's protection. It brought temporary safety but also plagues upon Pharaoh's house and led to their expulsion from Egypt. The pattern was seeded.

The next generation, **Isaac**, walks in his father's footsteps with startling precision. In Genesis 26:6-11, facing another famine, he settles in Gerar. The men of the place ask about his wife, Rebekah. "She is my sister," Isaac says, fearing for his life because she is beautiful. He replicates his father's deception almost verbatim. The same fear, the same method, the same potential for bringing defilement and judgment upon a foreign king, Abimelech. The pattern is not just remembered; it is re-enacted.

Then comes **Jacob**, the "heel-catcher," who takes the pattern and elevates it to an art form. In Genesis 27, he actively conspires with his mother to deceive his blind father, Isaac, in order to steal the birthright blessing from his brother Esau. He uses his father's favorite food, wears his brother's clothes, and covers his smooth skin with goat hides to perpetrate the fraud. This is no longer a fearful reaction to external circumstances; this is premeditated, proactive deception for personal gain. The pattern has matured from a defensive tactic to an offensive weapon.

Do you see the progression? From Abraham's fear-based half-truth, to Isaac's unthinking imitation, to Jacob's cunning and ambitious fraud. The core spirit—a spirit of Deception, of manipulating circumstances through untruth rather than trusting God's providence—remained constant. It was a behavioral and spiritual pattern woven deep into the bloodline, a familiar spirit that knew how to exploit the weakness in this family. It would continue to manifest in Jacob's sons, who would deceive him about the fate of Joseph, using the blood of a goat on a coat just as Jacob used the skin of a goat on his arms. The pattern echoed for generations.

This is the nature of a generational pattern. It is a river that has carved a deep channel through the landscape of a family's history. The water that flows down it may look slightly different each year, but it follows the same pre-cut path, eroding the same banks, unless a divine intervention dramatically redirects its course. Understanding this is the first step in wielding the authority to redirect that flow.

We now move from the subtle, often shape-shifting river of generational patterns to a more severe, specific, and legally potent manifestation: **Generational Curses**. If a pattern is a deep, eroded channel guiding the flow of behavior, a curse is a divine or demonic *decree* that actively dams the river, poisoning its waters and ensuring nothing downstream can flourish. It is a disempowering, limiting force of ancestral and generational connection that operates with the unyielding precision of a spiritual law.

A generational curse can be defined as a **limiting or disempowering force of ancestral and generational connection**. It is not merely a tendency or a learned behavior; it is a judicial sentence, a legally binding verdict in the spiritual realm that enforces the consequences of a forefather's specific, high-handed sin or, more potently, their covenant with darkness. Where a pattern suggests a familiar path, a curse erects an immovable wall. Where a pattern invites repetition, a curse enforces limitation.

The mechanism of a curse functions with the chilling efficiency of what the Apostle Paul termed "the law of sin and death" (Romans 8:2). It is a spiritual principle that, once activated, operates almost automatically, independent of the personal righteousness of subsequent generations. A curse draws invisible lines in the sand of a family's destiny. It puts up barriers in the realms of finance, health, relationships, and spiritual authority. A person laboring under a curse may strive with all their might, pray fervent prayers, and possess great skill, yet they consistently find themselves unable to cross a certain threshold. They are like a hamster on a wheel, running with all their strength but making no forward progress. The curse speaks a relentless, accusatory word over their life: "You cannot go beyond this point. This is your ceiling. This is your portion." It seeks to define an individual not based on their identity in Christ, not based on the calling of God on their life, but based on the failures, sins, and covenants of those who came before them. This is the practical, devastating outworking of Exodus 20:5—the iniquity of the fathers being visited upon the children, creating a spiritual environment of cursing rather than blessing.

To understand the tenacious, legally-binding nature of a spoken curse, we must examine a powerful biblical case study that spans generations: **The Curse on Jericho**.

In Joshua chapter 6, after the miraculous fall of Jericho's walls, Joshua, operating under divine inspiration, pronounces a solemn and specific oath:

"Cursed before the Lord be the man who rises up and rebuilds this city, Jericho. At the cost of his firstborn shall he lay its foundation, and at the cost of his youngest son shall he set up its gates." (Joshua 6:26)

This was not a casual statement of disapproval. This was a judicial curse uttered by a covenant leader with prophetic authority. It established a specific, negative inheritance for anyone arrogant or foolish enough to defy it. The curse was placed in the spiritual ledger over that location and over the bloodline of whoever would dare to challenge it.

Now, fast-forward approximately 500 years. We find ourselves in one of the darkest periods of Israel's history, during the reign of King Ahab, who, scripture tells us, did more to provoke the Lord to anger than all the kings of Israel before him (1 Kings 16:33). In 1 Kings 16:34, we read this stark and terrifying fulfillment:

"In his days Hiel of Bethel built Jericho. He laid its foundation at the cost of Abiram his firstborn, and set up its gates at the cost of his youngest son Segub, according to the word of the Lord, which he spoke by Joshua the son of Nun."

The text is chilling in its matter-of-fact delivery. Hiel of Bethel, in his pride or his ignorance, rebuilt Jericho. And the curse, dormant for half a millennium, activated with lethal precision. His firstborn son, Abiram, died when the foundation was laid. His youngest son, Segub, died when the gates were set up. The curse did not forget. It did not weaken with time. It did not care that Hiel may have been a skilled builder or had personal dreams for the city. The spiritual law, once decreed, executed its judgment exactly as prophesied.

This narrative demonstrates several critical principles about generational curses:

1. **Their Longevity:** A curse does not simply fade away with time. It remains legally binding until it is either fulfilled or definitively broken by a higher spiritual authority.
2. **Their Specificity:** The curse on Jericho was not a general "bad luck." It named the specific price: the firstborn and the youngest son. Generational curses in families can be equally specific—a certain type of loss, a particular age of death, a recurring financial amount that is always lost.
3. **Their Legal Standing:** The curse operated "according to the word of the Lord." It had divine sanction, showing that God Himself will enforce the consequences of words spoken by legitimate authority, even words of judgment. This is why curses spoken by parents, occult practitioners, or other authority figures carry such devastating power.
4. **Their Activation by Action:** Hiel's action of rebuilding was the trigger that released the full force of the curse. In families, certain actions, reaching certain milestones, or even speaking certain vows can activate dormant generational curses, releasing their limiting and disempowering power into a new generation.

A generational curse, therefore, is a spiritual shackle. It is the enemy's legal brief, citing the sins of your ancestors and the curses of Exodus and Deuteronomy, to argue before the court of heaven that you deserve limitation, sickness, and failure. It is a more aggressive and judicial form of spiritual oppression than a pattern, requiring not just awareness and resistance, but a specific, authoritative act of renunciation and breaking through the power of the Cross. To confuse a deep-seated curse with a simple pattern is to try to pick a bank vault's lock with a screwdriver; the tool is inadequate for the strength of the stronghold.

We come now to the third element in this taxonomy of torment, the mechanism that gives generational strongholds their eerie, predictable rhythm: **Generational Cycles**. If a pattern is the *what* (the specific behavior) and a curse is the *why* (the legal limitation), then a cycle is the *when*—the relentless, often timed, repetition of these negative events. It is the engine of repetition, the demonic timing belt that drives the pattern or curse with a precision that can feel like a spiritual law of physics.

A generational cycle can be defined as **the recurring, often rhythmic, nature of negative generational events.** It is the "Groundhog Day" effect within a bloodline, where history does not merely influence the present but appears to replicate itself with terrifying faithfulness. A cycle is not the event itself, but the *timetable* upon which the event occurs. It is the enemy's strategic plan to ensure that a family's history of trauma, loss, or failure does not remain a single point in the past but becomes a recurring line, a waveform of despair that crashes upon the shore of each generation at a predictable interval.

The manifestation of a cycle is often what causes people to feel a profound sense of fatalism. A family may experience a major financial crisis, a debilitating illness, or the breakdown of a key relationship like clockwork—every seven years, every ten years, or at a specific age that becomes a dreaded milestone. A cycle of debt, for instance, is not merely a pattern of poverty; it is the phenomenon where, just as financial breakthrough seems inevitable, a completely unexpected and catastrophic expense arises, wiping out savings and resetting the family's financial status to zero, again and again. It's as if an invisible hand pulls a lever at the precise moment of ascent, ensuring the family never escapes the gravitational pull of lack. A cycle of relational failure might see marriages consistently failing in the third or seventh year, regardless of the individuals involved. These are not coincidences; they are the footprints of a familiar spirit walking the same path on its assigned schedule.

The Biblical text provides us with a masterful and theologically rich case study of a generational cycle that threatened the very Messianic promise: **The Cycle of Barrenness and Delay.**

This cycle begins with **Sarah**, the wife of Abraham, the original recipient of the covenant promise. Genesis 11:30 states plainly, "Now Sarai was barren; she had no child." For twenty-five years, from the initial promise in Genesis 12 to its fulfillment in Genesis 21, the promise of a son was held in agonizing tension with the biological and spiritual reality of barrenness. The delay was not a passive waiting; it was an active, protracted struggle against a spiritual force that was resisting the purposes of God.

The cycle then repeats with striking similarity in the next generation. **Rebekah** is chosen as a wife for Isaac. The Bible immediately notes, "And Isaac prayed to the Lord for his wife, because she was barren" (Genesis 25:21). The same spirit of barrenness, the same delay, manifests again. It took twenty years of prayer and intercession before the cycle was broken and she conceived Jacob and Esau.

In the third generation, the cycle not only continues but intensifies in its complexity. **Jacob** is drawn to **Rachel**, and the scripture is unambiguous: "When the Lord saw that Leah was hated, he opened her womb, but Rachel was barren" (Genesis 29:31). Rachel's barrenness becomes a central drama of the narrative. Furthermore, Jacob's entire marital journey is fraught with the spirit of delay—deceived into working seven years for Leah, then obligated to work another seven for Rachel. The cyclical pattern of waiting and delay is woven into the very fabric of his story.

This triad of barrenness reveals the nature of a generational cycle:

1. **It Targets Destiny:** The cycle was not random. It was a strategic attack on the "seed," the Messianic line. The enemy understood the generational promise and focused his cyclical attack on the point of propagation.
2. **It Creates a Demonic Timetable:** The spirit of delay operated on a schedule—25 years, 20 years, years of waiting. It created a predictable rhythm of frustration.
3. **It Requires Specific Spiritual Intervention:** In each case, the cycle was not broken by passive waiting but by fervent, persistent prayer (Isaac), prophetic declaration (God's promise to Abraham), and spiritual warfare (Jacob's eventual blessing). The cycle had to be *disrupted* by a force greater than its own momentum.

Understanding the distinctions between Patterns, Curses, and Cycles is not an academic exercise; it is the very foundation of effective spiritual ministry. Misdiagnosis leads to misplaced effort and ministerial burnout.

- **Ministering to a Pattern** often requires **teaching and the renewal of the mind** (Romans 12:2). The deep channel of learned behavior must be redirected by filling the soul with the truth of God's Word, dismantling strongholds of thought, and learning new, godly responses. It is a process of discipleship and re-parenting in the Spirit.
- **Breaking a deep-seated Curse** requires the **authoritative application of the blood of Jesus and the renunciation of specific sins and covenants.** This is a judicial action. You are going before the court of heaven with the superior blood of Christ to nullify the legal claim of the curse. You must specifically renounce the sins of your fathers that opened the door, and you must declare the curse broken by the power of the Cross, severing its legal right to limit you.
- **Disrupting a persistent Cycle** often requires **strategic prayer and prophetic acts** to break the demonic timetable. This is like spiritual counter-intelligence. You must discern the rhythm of the attack and, through targeted fasting, prayer, and obedience to specific divine instructions (prophetic acts), you break the enemy's assigned schedule. You declare, "The cycle stops now! This timeline is broken in the name of Jesus! The spirit of delay is bound!"

These three—Pattern, Curse, and Cycle—are often intricately interwoven in a family line. A Curse of Poverty may create a Pattern of Financial Mismanagement, which operates on a Cycle of seven-year collapses. But a precise diagnosis is the first, and most critical, step toward a precise and powerful deliverance. You must know what you are fighting to wield the right weapon from the divine arsenal.

CHAPTER 06

The Generational God: Divine Principle and Diabolical Imitation

Beloved, we now arrive at the theological bedrock upon which this entire edifice of understanding is built. Every truth we have explored—every pattern, every curse, every cycle—rests upon a foundational reality so profound that to miss it is to render all subsequent deliverance unstable. It is this: **God is a generational God.** This is not merely an attribute among many; it is a fundamental aspect of His operational nature, the very way He has chosen to structure His relationship with creation and with humanity. To reject the concept of generational spiritual influence is not simply to disagree with a doctrine; it is to fundamentally misunderstand the heart and the methods of the Almighty. It is to look at a tree and deny the existence of its root system.

6.1 The Generational Nature of God

From the very inception of His covenant relationships, God's mind has operated on a transgenerational frequency. When He called Abram out of Ur of the Chaldeans, the promise He uttered was not a solitary, self-contained gift for one man. It was a seed designed to germinate across centuries. The divine declarations are unequivocal:

- **"To your offspring I will give this land."** (Genesis 12:7)
- **"For all the land that you see I will give to you and to your offspring forever. I will make your offspring as the dust of the earth."** (Genesis 13:15-16)
- **"And I will establish my covenant between me and you and your offspring after you throughout their generations for an everlasting covenant, to be God to you and to your offspring after you."** (Genesis 17:7-8)

The Hebrew word for "offspring" here, *zera*, means "seed." It is a collective noun pointing to a lineage, a succession, a continuous flow of descendants. God was not just promising land and nationhood to an elderly man; He was planting a nation in the loins of a single patriarch. The covenant was inherently, constitutionally generational.

This principle is so central to God's self-revelation that it becomes His signature, His chosen name in a moment of supreme theophany. At the burning bush, when Moses asks for the name of the God sending him, the reply is not a philosophical abstraction like "The Prime Mover" or "The Absolute." It is a name steeped in generational covenant: **"I am the God of your father, the God of Abraham, the God of**

Isaac, and the God of Jacob." (Exodus 3:6). In this one declaration, God inextricably links His own identity to a multi-generational legacy. He is not the God of the momentary encounter; He is the God of the unfolding story. He is the God who remembers His promises to Abraham while dealing with Isaac, and His faithfulness to Isaac while calling Jacob. The blessings of this covenant—divine protection in Egypt, supernatural provision in the wilderness, and prophetic purpose for a nation—did not terminate with Abraham. They flowed down the generational line like a mighty river, carrying Isaac, then Jacob, then the twelve tribes on their current.

This divine pattern is not relegated to the Old Testament, as if it were a primitive concept superseded by a more individualistic New Covenant. Absolutely not! The generational heart of God beats just as strongly in the New Testament, now expanded to a global scale. On the day of Pentecost, with the fire of the Holy Spirit freshly fallen, Peter stands to explain the phenomenon. And what is the scope of the promise he proclaims? He declares: **"For the promise is for you and for your children and for all who are far off, everyone whom the Lord our God calls to himself."** (Acts 2:39). The promise of the Holy Spirit, the very engine of the New Covenant, is explicitly framed in generational terms. It is "for you *and for your children*." God's redemptive plan in Christ does not think in terms of isolated individuals; it thinks in terms of **families and generations**. The Great Commission is to make disciples of *panta ta ethne*—all the nations, the *ethnos*, the people groups, which are by definition multi-generational entities.

This divine generational principle means that God's work is often a long-term project. He sows a promise in one generation that may not see its full harvest for three, four, or ten generations.

He can spare a wicked city, not for the sake of the wicked within it, but because of the righteous "seed" that is destined to come from it. He can answer the prayer of a sinner, not because of the sinner's merit, but because of the prophetic destiny attached to their bloodline. God is always playing the long game. He sees the end from the beginning, and His strategies are designed to unfold across the tapestry of time, weaving together the lives of grandparents, parents, and children into a single, glorious narrative of His faithfulness. To fail to understand this is to view God's activity through a keyhole, seeing only the immediate moment and missing the grand, sweeping epic of His generational purpose. This is the good and perfect pattern, the divine original, from which all else flows—and from which the enemy, in his malevolent genius, has created his most devastating perversion.

6.2 Satan as the Imitator

Having established the magnificent, life-giving truth of God's generational nature, we must now turn our gaze to the sinister shadow it casts. For in the spiritual realm, there exists a brutal and unyielding law: every divine original has a demonic counterfeit. The enemy of our souls, Satan, is the supreme imitator. We must be absolutely clear on this foundational truth: **Satan possesses no creative power.** He is not a co-creator. He is a created being, a fallen cherub, whose original brilliance and beauty, described in Ezekiel 28:12-15, were given to him by God. His rebellion, detailed in Isaiah 14:12-15, was an act of prideful will, not creative genius. His entire kingdom operates on a single, parasitic principle: he can only corrupt, pervert, twist, and imitate what God has already created.

Having studied the generational nature of God's covenant dealings for millennia, observing how God so masterfully uses family lines as conduits for blessing, identity, and redemption, Satan established his own demonic counterpart: **generational curses.** This is the dark mirror. Just as God uses the river of a bloodline to carry the water of life to successive generations, Satan works to poison that same river at its source, ensuring it carries a toxin of death, sin, and destruction to everyone downstream. He understands the legal and spiritual architecture of the family unit—the concept of covenant headship, the power of a father's words and actions, the vulnerability of children—and he exploits it with ruthless efficiency. If God's method is to establish a "God of Abraham, Isaac, and Jacob," Satan's method is to establish a "spirit of fear, addiction, and poverty" over a Smith, a Jones, or a Johnson lineage.

This is where the **"law of balance"** I have articulated in my ministry becomes a critical hermeneutical key. This is not a man-made concept; it is a principle derived from the consistent witness of Scripture. One cannot, with any theological integrity, affirm the reality of generational blessings while simultaneously denying the possibility of generational curses. To do so is to embrace a lopsided, selectively optimistic theology that has no basis in the full counsel of God. They are two sides of the same spiritual coin. How can you define "light" if you refuse to acknowledge the existence of "darkness"? How can you comprehend "healing" if you reject the reality of "sickness"? How can you preach an "up" if there is no "down"?

Moses presented this very choice to Israel in Deuteronomy 11:26-28: **"See, I am setting before you today a blessing and a curse: the blessing, if you obey the commandments of the Lord your God... and the curse, if you do not obey the**

commandments of the Lord your God." The blessing and the curse exist in the same spiritual ecosystem, governed by the same covenant. They are the two potential outcomes of a single relationship. To believe in one is to logically and biblically accept the potential of the other.

This understanding is not dualism—the belief in two equal and opposing ultimate powers. That is a heresy. God is the only uncreated, omnipotent Being. Satan is a defeated foe, a created being whose time is short. This, instead, is the recognition that **Satan's kingdom is a parasitic, inverted mirror of the Kingdom of God.** It has no substance of its own. It is a photographic negative of the divine original. Where God has priesthood, Satan has a occult hierarchy. Where God has the communion table, Satan has ritual sacrifices. Where God has the blood of Jesus for cleansing, Satan demands blood sacrifices for defilement. And where God has generational blessings flowing through covenant faithfulness, Satan has generational curses flowing through covenant-breaking sin. His entire operation is a grotesque imitation, a stolen blueprint used to build a prison instead of a palace.

Therefore, when you see a generational pattern of destruction in a family, you are not seeing the creative power of the devil. You are seeing his parasitic perversion of God's good design for generational legacy. He has hijacked the delivery system God intended for blessing and is using it to deliver a package of death. But praise be to God, the One who designed the system is also the One who provided the means to reclaim it, to exorcise the parasite, and to restore the flow of blessing. To understand this diabolical imitation is to understand the enemy's strategy, and to understand his strategy is the first step in dismantling it completely.

6.3 The Sinner and the Generational Answer

We now come to a facet of God's generational nature that should both stagger our understanding and revolutionize our sense of purpose. The Almighty's calculus is not confined to the immediate moment or the isolated individual. An illuminating, often overlooked aspect of His sovereignty is this: **God can extend mercy, grant reprieve, or even answer a prayer not for the sake of the individual petitioner, but for the sake of a generation yet unborn.** His decisions in the present are often dictated by His purposes for the future, revealing a strategic depth to His grace that transcends our limited, individualistic perspective.

We see this principle operative in the divine deliberation over Sodom. Abraham intercedes, bargaining for the city, and the Lord agrees that if even ten righteous people can be found, He will spare the entire metropolis for their sake (Genesis 18:32). The mercy shown is not for the benefit of the wicked majority, but for the sake of the righteous minority and the potential destiny contained within them. This is not an isolated incident. God can stay His hand of judgment on a wicked nation because He knows that a prophet, a reformer, or a godly lineage is destined to emerge from it generations later. He may providentially answer the prayer of an unbeliever—for healing, for provision, for rescue—not because that person stands in a right covenant relationship with Him, but because that answered prayer will create a critical pathway, preserve a specific bloodline, or open a necessary door for a future move of God that will bring multitudes into His kingdom. The sinner becomes, often unknowingly, a steward of a grace that is intended for their descendants. God is, in essence, answering the prayer of a future generation in the present, using the current individual as the vessel for that answer.

This divine perspective dramatically reframes our understanding of our own lives. It demonstrates that **God's primary focus is not merely the individual in a vacuum, but the individual as a link in a chain of destiny.** You are not a solitary actor on the stage of life. You are a critical nexus point between your past and your future. The choices you make, the prayers you pray, the battles you fight, and the obedience you offer today are not just about your personal comfort or your immediate circumstances. They are about shaping the spiritual inheritance of your children, your grandchildren, and your great-grandchildren. You are either reinforcing the enemy's strongholds or you are dismantling them for the generations to come.

This understanding should instill in every believer a profound, holy, and weighty sense of **responsibility**. Your obedience today is not a small, private matter. When you choose to forgive a deep wound instead of passing on a spirit of bitterness, you are not just freeing yourself—you are severing a chain of hatred that could have tormented your lineage for a hundred years. When you break a pattern of addiction through the power of the Spirit, you are not just achieving personal victory—you are slamming shut a door of hell that has stood open in your family for generations. When you stand in prayer and renounce the sins of your fathers and plead the blood of Jesus over your bloodline, you are engaging in a prophetic act that redeems the past and sanctifies the future. Your faithfulness can be the turning point, the "thus far and no further" decree that breaks a chain of cursing that has persisted for centuries and releases a legacy of blessing for your children's children. You have the potential to become the "Abraham" of your family—the one who heard God's call to leave the old, cursed "father's house" and step into a new covenant destiny.

Conversely, this revelation casts a stark light on the ferocity of our spiritual opposition. It reveals why the enemy fights with such vicious, relentless intensity to maintain his generational strongholds in your life. He is not just fighting *you*—your personal comfort, your individual success. **He is fighting a potential legacy.** He sees in your spirit the seed of a godly generation. He knows that if you break through, you will not come out alone. You will lead your entire household—present and future—out of his dominion and into the glorious liberty of the children of God (Acts 16:31). He is not just trying to make you miserable; he is trying to prevent the birth of reformers, prophets, and kings who will carry the gospel to nations. Your struggle is not small. The weight of generations rests upon your obedience. The enemy knows the generational principle better than many believers do, and he trembles at the potential of one anointed, awakened "link" who, by the power of the Spirit, can shatter the chain that has held his captives for so long.

CHAPTER 07

The Primacy of the Father's Blood

Beloved, we now drill down into one of the most pivotal and, for some, contentious revelations in this entire study. Within the divinely ordained generational structure, Scripture consistently assigns a particular and profound primacy to the **father's bloodline**. I must be exceedingly clear from the outset: this is not to diminish or devalue the immense influence of the mother, whose biological, emotional, and spiritual contribution is indispensable and powerful in its own right. Rather, it is to recognize and submit to the biblical and spiritual principle of **paternal headship**—a principle that God established as a foundational covenant reality, and one that operates with equal force in the realms of both blessing and cursing. The father, in the divine economy, functions as the covenant head, the priestly representative, and the spiritual governor of his household. His actions, his words, and his blood, therefore, carry a unique weight of authority and consequence that sets the spiritual trajectory for his descendants.

7.1 The Biological and Spiritual Transmission

To understand this, we must begin at the most fundamental level: the moment of conception. From a biological standpoint, the miracle of human life is initiated by the union of two sets of genetic information. A child receives 23 chromosomes from the mother and 23 chromosomes from the father. This is a scientific fact, but it is also a spiritual parable. The father's blood, carrying its unique genetic code—its record of ancestral strengths, weaknesses, predispositions, and physical traits—is a 50% contributor to the child's biological and spiritual makeup from the very instant of their existence. The child is not a blank slate; they are a living amalgamation of two deep, ancient rivers of heredity.

This biological reality finds its spiritual corollary in the poignant confession of King David. In Psalm 51:5, after his grievous sin with Bathsheba, he cries out to God, **"Behold, I was brought forth in iniquity, and in sin did my mother conceive me."** For centuries, this verse has been misunderstood. David is not confessing some illicit sexual act surrounding his own conception. He is not accusing his mother, the righteous Jesse, of sin. No, he is operating under a profound spirit of revelation, acknowledging a spiritual law that transcends his personal actions. He is declaring that from the very moment of his biological origin, from the instant the blood of his father Jesse and the womb of his mother came together, he was already embedded in a sinful lineage. He inherited a fallen nature, a spiritual predisposition to sin, transmitted through the blood of his father, which itself was part of the unbroken, corrupted stream flowing all the way back to Adam. The "iniquity" and "sin" he references are corporate, ancestral realities. He was conceived into a state of spiritual separation, not because of what he had done, but because of the nature of the blood that gave him life. His human spirit was, at birth, already tuned to the frequency of the Adamic fall.

This is the very reason why the **Virgin Birth of our Lord Jesus Christ was absolutely non-negotiable.** It was not a mere display of divine power or a theological novelty. It was a soteriological necessity of the highest order. Had Joseph been the biological father of Jesus, had the conception occurred through natural means, Jesus would have inevitably inherited the sin nature of Adam, carried by Joseph's blood. The taint was in the bloodline itself. The voice of Joseph's blood, which echoed with the sins of David, of Jacob, of Isaac, of Abraham, and ultimately of Adam, would have been the voice speaking in the veins of the Messiah. He would have been born a sinner, needing a savior Himself, and utterly disqualified from being the spotless Lamb of God who takes away the sin of the world (John 1:29).

But, hallelujah, the Gospel records the divine interruption of this cursed cycle! Jesus was conceived not by the will of man, nor by the blood of man, but by the overshadowing power of the Holy Spirit in the womb of the Virgin Mary (Luke 1:35). The life that began to grow was not fertilized by the seed of a fallen man. The blood that began to form in the embryonic Savior was entirely new, uncreated, divine blood. It was a holy, untainted river sprung forth in the desert of fallen humanity. His blood carried no record of Adam's rebellion, no testimony of David's adultery, no echo of Jacob's deception. His blood was pure, its only witness being to the perfect, righteous nature of God the Father. This is why He could ask, "Which of you convicts me of sin?" (John 8:46). The hematological evidence was perfect. The witness of His blood testified only to purity, making Him the only suitable sacrifice to satisfy the legal demand of the law and to silence forever the condemning voice of the old, Adamic bloodline for all who are in Him.

7.2 The Father's Blood as the Primary Enemy of Destiny

I now make a statement that may sound radical, even shocking, to the uninstructed ear, but one that emerges with stark clarity from a holistic reading of Scripture and the hard-won wisdom of deliverance ministry: **"The number one enemy of every child of Destiny is their father's blood."** This is not a statement of disrespect toward fathers, nor a dismissal of their God-given role. It is a sober, biblically supportable diagnosis of the primary stronghold that must be overcome to step into a God-ordained future. The father, occupying the position of covenant head over the family, functions as the spiritual rudder of the household vessel. His sins, his unrenounced covenants, his soul wounds, and his ingrained iniquities do not merely affect him; they create a pervasive spiritual atmosphere—a "father's house"—that can become an invisible prison, a confining identity, and a limiting destiny for his descendants.

This is not a matter of personal animosity, but of spiritual law. The father's blood, as we have established, is a witness. When that blood carries the record of idolatry, addiction, fear, or rebellion, it testifies against his children. It speaks a word of limitation over their future. It says, "This is your ceiling. This is your inheritance. This is who you are." The enemy, the accuser, uses this testimony as his primary legal brief to oppose the child of destiny, arguing before the courts of heaven that they are defined by their father's failures and are therefore disqualified from their God-given purpose.

This profound spiritual dynamic is powerfully and paradigmatically illustrated in the divine call of Abram. God's command in Genesis 12:1 is meticulously structured in three ascending levels of separation: **"Go from your country and your kindred and your father's house."**

- **Your Country:** This is the outermost circle—the geographical location, the national culture, the external environment. One can emigrate from South Africa to the United Kingdom and change their country.
- **Your Kindred:** This is the second circle—the extended family network, the clan, the social and relational pressures of one's lineage. One can distance themselves from troublesome relatives and leave their kindred.
- **Your Father's House:** This is the innermost and most potent circle. This phrase signifies infinitely more than a physical dwelling. It represents the **spiritual atmosphere, the bloodline inheritance, the limitations, and the core identity defined by the father.** The "house" of Terah was, according to Joshua 24:2, a house of idolatry. It was a spiritual ecosystem where false gods were served, where covenants with demons were in place, and where a limited, pagan identity was imposed.

The critical revelation here is this: **you can leave your country and your kindred and yet remain fully within your "father's house."** You can move from Angola to Spain, you can cut off all contact with your extended family, but if you have not spiritually exited the "father's house"—if you have not broken the power of the generational curses, patterns, and identities carried by your father's blood—you will simply recreate the same problems in a new location. You will be in a new nation, but you will still be living in the spiritual confines of Terah's house. The poverty, the sickness, the relational dysfunction, the spiritual blindness—they will all follow you, because you carried them with you in your blood.

The biblical narrative provides the proof. Abram had two biological brothers: Nahor and Haran. They remained in Ur, in the "father's house" of Terah. They remained in the geographical location and under the direct spiritual covering of their idolatrous father. And what became of them? They faded into utter historical irrelevance. Their names are mere footnotes in the genealogical record. They were consumed by the spiritual atmosphere of their father's house.

Abram, however, by obeying God's command to the letter, exited not just physically but *spiritually*. His obedience was an act of violent disconnection from the spiritual DNA of his father. It was a declaration that his identity and destiny would no longer be defined by Terah's idolatry, but by Yahweh's promise. By exiting his father's house, Abram broke the power of the idolatrous bloodline over his life and destiny. He severed the legal claim that the enemy had over him through his father's covenants. His obedience did not just change his location; it changed his spiritual parentage and unleashed a generational blessing that would flow to all nations.

This is the exact warfare you are engaged in. Your "Terah" may be a spirit of poverty, a legacy of addiction, a stronghold of fear, or a covenant with disease. Your father's blood is speaking that identity over you. But God is calling you, as He called Abram, to "go out from your father's house." This is not a physical command for most, but a spiritual one: a decisive, authoritative renunciation and breaking, in the name of Jesus, of every ungodly inheritance passed down through your father's bloodline. It is the only way to step out of the shadow of that house and into the limitless destiny God has for you.

7.3 The Blood's Power of Attraction

We now venture into one of the most subtle, yet most powerful, manifestations of the blood's testimony: its uncanny, often destructive, **power of attraction**. The father's blood does not merely speak a word of limitation from within; it actively shapes the external environment and relationships of the descendant, functioning as a spiritual magnet that draws circumstances and people that will reinforce its own familiar, fallen narrative. This is not about fate or karma; it is about the blood's witness creating a spiritual frequency to which demonic forces and susceptible individuals resonate, orchestrating events to fulfill the bloodline's self-prophecy.

This phenomenon is masterfully illustrated in the intergenerational saga of the patriarchs, specifically in the choice of wives—a decision of paramount importance for the covenant line. Let us trace this pattern with the meticulous eye of a spiritual investigator.

It begins with **Abraham**. His wife, **Sarah**, is described in Scripture in ways that highlight two key characteristics. First, she is repeatedly noted for her striking physical beauty. When taken to Egypt, the princes of Pharaoh praise her to him, and she is taken into his palace because of her appearance (Genesis 12:14-15). Second, and more critically, the text is unequivocal about her condition: **"Now Sarai was barren; she had no child."** (Genesis 11:30). She was beautiful and barren.

When the time comes for a wife for the next generation, Abraham, now the covenant head, gives his senior servant a specific charge to find a wife for Isaac from his own kindred. The servant, guided by God, finds **Rebekah**. And how is she described? The text is strikingly specific: **"The young woman was very attractive in appearance, a maiden whom no man had known."** (Genesis 24:16). She is, like Sarah, notably beautiful. And then, with the same devastating precision as with Sarah, the narrative soon reveals: **"And Isaac prayed to the Lord for his wife, because she was barren."** (Genesis 25:21). The pattern holds: beautiful and barren.

The cycle intensifies in the third generation. **Isaac** and Rebekah have a son, **Jacob**. When Jacob meets **Rachel**, the scripture records his reaction and her description: **"Now Rachel was beautiful of form and countenance."** (Genesis 29:17). Jacob is immediately, powerfully drawn to her. And, as if following a pre-written script, the biblical record soon states: **"When the Lord saw that Leah was hated, he opened her womb, but Rachel was barren."** (Genesis 29:31). For the third time, the chosen matriarch is characterized by exceptional beauty and the affliction of barrenness.

To dismiss this as a series of coincidences or a mere cultural preference for beauty is to be willfully blind to the spiritual pattern screaming from the text. This is more than happenstance. This is the **bloodline, carrying the specific pattern of barrenness and a deeply ingrained "preference" for a physical type that mirrored the original mother, actively influencing the choice of wives.** The blood was speaking. It was attracting. It was dictating terms to ensure the continuation of its own familiar testimony of delay and struggle. It was as if the blood in Isaac's veins recognized in Rebekah a familiar spiritual and even physical "echo" of his mother Sarah, and was drawn to it. The same force was at work in Jacob, pulling him irresistibly toward a woman who, like his grandmother, was beautiful and barren.

This is the power of attraction inherent in a generational stronghold. It is not that the individuals lacked free will; it is that their affections, their desires, their very "type" was being powerfully shaped by an unseen force working through the record in their blood. The enemy, exploiting the legal ground of the barrenness pattern, was able to influence their choices to ensure the curse continued. The blood was a conspirator with the enemy, whispering, "This is the one you should desire. This feels right. This is familiar."

This revelation brings a terrifying and liberating clarity. It demonstrates with brutal force why mere willpower, positive thinking, and sheer determination are so often utterly insufficient to break deep generational patterns. You can *want* a healthy relationship, but if the blood in your veins is testifying to a pattern of rejection and abuse, it will unconsciously attract you to rejecting and abusive partners. You can *desire* financial freedom, but if the blood carries a witness of poverty and loss, it will orchestrate circumstances that lead to sudden, inexplicable financial collapse. You are not just fighting a bad habit; you are fighting a voice in your own body, a familiar spirit that knows the "you" that your blood remembers, and is working tirelessly to make that identity a present reality.

The blood's power of attraction is perhaps the most insidious of its operations, because it makes you a willing participant in your own bondage. It makes the familiar feel like home, even when that home is a prison. But this is also where the victory of Christ is most profoundly felt. For the blood of Jesus does not just silence the old testimony; it rewires our spiritual and soulish affections. It breaks the demonic magnetism of the curse and gives us a new "frequency" of attraction—toward life, toward health, toward wholeness, and toward relationships that build up rather than tear down. The superior testimony of the Lamb's blood can reset the entire relational and circumstantial gravitational pull of your life, freeing you from the unconscious conspiracy of your own inheritance.

CHAPTER 08

Case Study in Genesis: The Patriarchal Bloodline and the Pattern of Barrenness

Beloved, we now turn from theoretical frameworks to a living, breathing case study etched into the very foundation of our faith. The book of Genesis provides us with a masterful, divinely-inspired laboratory in which to observe the operation of a generational pattern with terrifying clarity. The recurring, agonizing issue of barrenness among the matriarchs is not a random collection of unfortunate biological events, nor is it a mere literary device. It is a clear, traceable, and strategic bloodline stronghold—a specific generational pattern that Satan, the accuser, wielded like a precise weapon in a desperate attempt to sever the Messianic promise at its root before it could ever bear fruit. In this living narrative, we see the nature of spiritual warfare over destiny, the patience of God's promise, and the ultimate triumph of covenant over curse.

8.1 The Pattern Established: Sarah

The pattern is established with stark, unadorned finality in the scriptural record. Genesis 11:30 offers no explanation, no backstory, no mitigating circumstances. It simply states a brute, devastating fact: **"Now Sarai was barren; she had no child."** The Hebrew is even more emphatic and poetic in its tragedy: *`aqarah hi' welad lain lah*—"Barren she was; child there was not to her." The construction underscores a state of being, an established and seemingly fixed reality.

It is profoundly significant to note the specific language used here. Contrast this with the later account of Hannah, another barren woman, where the text explicitly states, **"because the Lord had closed her womb."** (1 Samuel 1:5-6). In Hannah's case, the barrenness is presented as a specific, sovereign act of God for a prophetic purpose, a temporary condition that would set the stage for a dramatic answer to prayer and the birth of a prophet. For Sarah, no such divine agency is cited. Her barrenness is presented as her inherent condition, a foundational part of her biological and spiritual identity from the very beginning of her recorded history.

This is a critical distinction. Sarah's barrenness was not a divinely imposed pause; it was a manifestation of a **pre-existing spiritual reality embedded in her bloodline**. She came from the same "father's house" as Abraham—the house of Terah, the idolater. She was a daughter of Ur of the Chaldeans, a center of moon-god worship. Her barrenness was a feature, a symptom, of that cursed spiritual ecosystem. It was part of the "old creation" package that needed to be overcome by the "new creation" promise of God. The enemy, understanding the cosmic stakes of the seed promised to Abraham (Genesis 3:15), had established a stronghold of fruitlessness in the very line through which the Deliverer was to come.

For twenty-five excruciating years, from the initial promise in Genesis 12 to its fulfillment in Genesis 21, the supernatural promise of God concerning a son was held in agonizing tension with this unyielding biological and spiritual reality. Every sunrise that passed without a child was a taunt from the enemy, a whisper that the bloodline's testimony of barrenness was stronger than the word of the covenant God. Every cultural expectation, every personal hope deferred, was a pressure point exploited by the spirit of delay. During this period, we see the fruit of this tension: human efforts to circumvent the problem, leading to the birth of Ishmael through Hagar, an event that itself spawned a generational conflict that persists to this day. The pattern was not passive; it was an active, oppressive force that provoked fear, impatience, and covenant-breaking solutions.

Sarah's barrenness, therefore, stands as the archetype. It represents the **foundational stronghold** that must be confronted and broken. It shows us that the promises of God do not automatically erase generational patterns; rather, they enter into direct conflict with them, creating a spiritual battlefield in the life of the believer. The victory does not come from ignoring the pattern or devising human schemes, but from a persistent, tenacious faith that eventually partners with God's power to perform a creative miracle that shatters the pattern's very foundation. Sarah's womb, dead to the natural order for nine decades, became the ground zero where the word of God finally overpowered the testimony of the bloodline, demonstrating that no curse, no pattern, and no delay can ultimately thwart the purposes of the Almighty for those who believe.

8.2 The Pattern Repeated: Rebekah

The generational pattern, having been firmly established in the foundational generation, now demonstrates its terrifying tenacity and precision in the next. The narrative moves from Abraham and Sarah to their son, Isaac, and his wife, Rebekah. The transition is seamless, and the recurrence of the stronghold is recorded with a stark, matter-of-fact tone that underscores its inevitability apart from divine intervention. The scripture states, with no fanfare or surprise, **"And Isaac prayed to the Lord for his wife, because she was barren."** (Genesis 25:21).

This single verse is a universe of theological and practical insight into the nature of generational patterns. First, it confirms that the pattern did not skip a generation. The spirit of barrenness and delay that had afflicted Sarah did not simply dissipate with the death of the previous generation or the inauguration of the covenant through Isaac. The stronghold was not personal to Sarah; it was attached to the *bloodline*, to the covenant family itself. The enemy's legal claim, established in the "father's house" of Terah and reinforced by the decades of delay with Abraham and Sarah, remained active and sought to express itself in the next logical vessel: the wife of the covenant heir.

Second, the text reveals the mechanism of transmission and the required response. Rebekah's barrenness was not described as an inherent condition from her birth, as it was with Sarah. She was chosen from Abraham's kin in Mesopotamia, brought into the covenant family by faith and divine guidance. Yet, upon her union with Isaac—the merging of her life with the Abrahamic bloodline that carried this pattern—the stronghold manifested. This illustrates a profound principle: **entering into covenant with a bloodline means coming under the influence of both its blessings and its burdens.** The spiritual ecosystem of Isaac's life, shaped by his father's legacy, created an environment where the familiar spirit of barrenness could legally operate against his wife. The blood was speaking, and its testimony was one of delay.

Third, and most critically, we see the nature of the battle required to break the pattern. The text does not say that Isaac simply waited. It says **"Isaac prayed..."** The Hebrew word used here, *`athar*, is significant. It means to plead, to entreat, to interpose. It implies earnest, persistent, and likely repeated supplication. This was not a one-time, passive prayer. This was spiritual warfare. For **twenty years**, Isaac stood in the gap, interceding for his wife, contending against the spiritual force that was resisting the fulfillment of God's promise to multiply Abraham's seed.

This twenty-year period is a critical detail. It shows that the breaking of a generational pattern is often not an instantaneous event, but a process of sustained spiritual pressure. It requires perseverance in prayer and faith. The spirit of delay, a key component of this stronghold, is designed to wear down the believer, to create discouragement, and to provoke, as it did with Abraham, human-engineered solutions. Isaac did not resort to taking a concubine. He pressed into prayer. His intercession was the spiritual weapon that slowly, over two decades, wore down the legal foundations of the curse and created the spiritual atmosphere for a miracle.

The pattern repeated, but the response was different. Abraham's journey involved a mixture of faith and fleshly effort (Ishmael). Isaac's story shows a progression: a focused, persistent, prayerful confrontation of the stronghold. The victory, when it came—the conception of Jacob and Esau—was therefore a direct result of spiritual warfare. It demonstrated that while generational patterns are powerful and persistent, they are not invincible. They yield to the consistent, faith-filled application of spiritual authority and intercession, proving that the power of a praying covenant partner can disrupt the enemy's timetable and release the purposes of God into a bloodline.

8.3 The Pattern Intensified: Rachel

In the third generation, the demonic pattern of barrenness does not merely repeat; it metastasizes, intensifying in both its emotional complexity and its strategic entanglement with other familial strongholds. The narrative shifts to Jacob, the son of Isaac and Rebekah, and the stage is set in the household of his uncle Laban. Here, the pattern manifests with a virulence that reveals the enemy's escalating desperation to thwart the Messianic line.

Jacob's initial encounter with Rachel is one of immediate, powerful attraction. The scripture emphasizes her appeal, noting she was **"beautiful in form and appearance"** (Genesis 29:17). This description, echoing the beauty of Sarah and Rebekah, is the first clue that the familiar spiritual magnet of the bloodline is activating once more. However, the subsequent revelation is devastating in its predictability. After Jacob is tricked into marrying Leah first, the biblical record delivers the blow: **"When the Lord saw that Leah was hated, he opened her womb, but Rachel was barren."** (Genesis 29:31). The contrast is deliberate and stark. Leah, the unloved wife, is granted fertility, while Rachel, the beloved, is gripped by the same spirit of barrenness that plagued her husband's grandmother and mother-in-law. Rachel's barrenness becomes a central, agonizing drama of the narrative, fueling a bitter rivalry with her sister and provoking the desperate cry, **"Give me children, or I shall die!"** (Genesis 30:1). The emotional and relational devastation wrought by the pattern is now fully visible.

But the intensification of the pattern is not limited to Rachel's womb. Jacob's entire marital journey is itself a masterpiece of delay and deception, mirroring and amplifying the struggles of his forefathers. He works seven years for Rachel, only to be deceived by Laban and given Leah instead. He is then forced to work *another* seven years for the wife he originally desired. This fourteen-year period of labor and waiting is a direct manifestation of the **spirit of delay** that is a core component of the generational stronghold. Just as Abraham and Sarah waited 25 years, and Isaac and Rebekah waited 20 years, Jacob now endures a 14-year postponement of his full marital destiny. The pattern has expanded its domain from biological reproduction to the very timing and fulfillment of covenant relationships.

Furthermore, this generation sees the pattern intertwining with the other powerful stronghold in the bloodline: **deception**. Jacob, the "heel-catcher," who himself deceived his father and brother, now becomes the victim of a more cunning deceiver in Laban. The generational iniquity is now operating in a feedback loop: the deception in the bloodline creates the circumstances for the delay, and the delay exacerbates the relational strife that fuels further sin. The enemy is no longer just attacking one front; he is ensnaring the entire family system in a web of interconnected curses.

This intensification reveals a critical spiritual principle: **unbroken generational patterns gain strength and complexity over time.** They become more deeply embedded in the family's soul life, affecting more areas of existence, and becoming more resistant to simple solutions. The cry of Rachel is the cry of a generation that has inherited a battle they did not start, facing a giant that has been fed and strengthened by the choices of their ancestors. It shows that the enemy's strategy is adaptive and relentless. Yet, even in this intensified state, the pattern is not invincible. It still yields, as we will see, to the persistent, if sometimes flawed, faith of God's people and His sovereign determination to fulfill His covenant promises. The stage is now set for the ultimate confrontation between this entrenched curse and the redemptive power of a covenant-keeping God.

8.4 Theological Implications of the Pattern

This harrowing triad of barrenness—stretching across three generations from Sarah to Rebekah to Rachel—is not merely a historical record of personal family tragedy. It is a divine revelation, a masterclass in spiritual dynamics that unveils several non-negotiable, foundational principles for understanding and overcoming generational strongholds. The Holy Spirit has preserved this narrative not as an artifact, but as a living, breathing textbook on spiritual warfare at the bloodline level.

First, this case study demonstrates with brutal clarity that Bloodline Patterns are Persistently Tenacious. They possess a demonic staying power that does not automatically disappear, even when operating under the most powerful covenant of blessing ever established. Consider the context: Abraham was the friend of God, the recipient of an unconditional, earth-shaking covenant promise that his seed would be as numerous as the stars. Isaac was the child of promise, the miraculous son through whom the covenant was to be established. Jacob was chosen by God before birth, the recipient of the Abrahamic blessing. Yet, the pattern of barrenness did not care. It respected neither their personal righteousness, their covenant status, nor their divine calling. It was a spiritual law of death operating with grim consistency within the very family chosen to bring forth life. This shatters the naive assumption that being "in covenant" or being a "child of promise" automatically immunizes one from generational strongholds. The legal ground established by the "father's house" of Terah provided a beachhead for the enemy that had to be consciously and aggressively contested, even by those walking in the highest levels of divine purpose.

Second, we see that these Persistent Patterns Require Specific, Targeted Intervention. In each generation, the pattern was not broken by passive waiting, wishful thinking, or the mere passage of time. It was shattered by a deliberate, forceful application of spiritual authority. The methodology of deliverance was tailored, showing us that there is no one-size-fits-all approach. For Abraham and Sarah, the key was **Prophetic Declaration**—the relentless standing on the specific, spoken word of God against all visible contradiction for twenty-five years. Their faith was not passive; it was an active force that held fast to the promise until it materialized. For Isaac and Rebekah, the weapon was **Fervent, Persistent Prayer**—a twenty-year campaign of intercession where Isaac *`athar*—pleaded and entreated—God on behalf of his wife. This was spiritual labor, a violent pressing into the kingdom of heaven that would not take no for an answer. In Jacob's generation, we see a complex form of **Spiritual Warfare and Sovereignty**—a combination of Rachel's desperate cry, the use of prophetic mandrakes (a point of faith mixed with superstition), and ultimately God's sovereign remembrance of Rachel that finally opened her womb. The pattern yielded only when confronted with a force greater than its own inertia.

Third, and most critically, this narrative reveals Satan's Strategic Target. The pattern of barrenness was not a random affliction. It was a precise, calculated, and sustained spiritual attack on the "seed"—the Messianic line promised in Genesis 3:15. Satan, the ancient serpent, understood the generational nature of God's promise better than many believers do today. He knew that if he could stop the seed, he could stop the Savior. He knew that if he could inflict barrenness upon the matriarchs, he could strangle the redemptive plan in its cradle. This reveals a terrifying and glorious truth: **generational curses are often strategically placed at the most vulnerable points of divine destiny.** The enemy does not waste his ammunition on trivialities. He studies the blueprints of God's purpose for a family and then lays siege to the very thing that would most advance the Kingdom—be it a calling to ministry, a gift of healing, a legacy of financial stewardship, or a destiny of leadership. The struggle you face may feel personal, but it is likely strategic. You are fighting not just for your own peace, but for the survival of a God-given destiny in your bloodline.

This Genesis case study, therefore, provides the ultimate biblical precedent for identifying and addressing multi-generational strongholds. It gives us permission, and indeed a mandate, to look beyond our immediate circumstances and our personal failures to see the larger spiritual war being waged over our lineage. It shows that what is happening in your life today—that recurring struggle, that persistent failure, that inexplicable delay—may not be about you personally. You may simply be the present-day battlefield in a long-standing spiritual war over your bloodline. You are the latest soldier in a conflict that began with your ancestors. But the glorious corollary is this: **you are also the one who can turn the tide.** The pattern can be broken. The curse can be reversed. But it will not happen by accident. It requires a profound understanding of its ancient origin, a ruthless diagnosis of its present manifestation, and a deliberate, authoritative application of the redemptive power of the Lord Jesus Christ, who became a curse for us to redeem us from the curse of the law (Galatians 3:13). Your life is the point of contact where the finished work of the Cross can finally, decisively, silence the ancient voice of the curse and release your bloodline into its God-ordained destiny.

CHAPTER 09

The Blood of Abel vs. The Blood of Jesus: A Typological Analysis

Beloved, we now arrive at the supreme climax of our entire study, the pivotal point upon which all deliverance from generational iniquity turns. The foundational conflict between the condemning voice of the old, Adamic bloodline and the liberating voice of the new covenant is masterfully and eternally illustrated in the stark, typological contrast between two bloods: the blood of Abel and the blood of Jesus Christ. This is not a minor theological comparison; it is the central dichotomy of redemption, the ultimate courtroom drama where two witnesses present opposing testimonies about your life and your lineage. To understand this dichotomy is to grasp the very mechanics of how we are translated from the kingdom of darkness into the kingdom of God's beloved Son.

9.1 The Cry of Abel's Blood: The Voice of the Old Covenant

We must begin where the terrible chorus of condemnation first began. As we have previously established in Genesis 4:10, after Cain murdered his brother Abel, God Himself confronts the first murderer with a declaration that would echo through every subsequent generation: **"The voice of your brother's blood cries out to me from the ground."** We must not rush past this. The blood of Abel, the first human to die, was not silent. It was a witness. It had a voice. And the content of its cry, as revealed by the context of God's response to Cain, was not a cry for mercy, nor a whisper of forgiveness. It was a piercing, unrelenting, judicial cry for **justice and vengeance.**

God's full statement makes this unequivocal: **"What have you done? The voice of your brother's blood cries out to me from the ground. And now you are cursed from the ground, which has opened its mouth to receive your brother's blood from your hand."** (Genesis 4:10-11). The blood's cry resulted in a curse. It demanded retribution according to the strict, unyielding principle of *lex talionis*—the law of equivalent retaliation embedded later in the Mosaic code: **"life for life, eye for eye, tooth for tooth..."** (Exodus 21:23-24). Abel's blood, spilled in righteous innocence, cried out for Cain's life in return. It was the voice of the law in its purest, most severe form: the law of sin and death.

This voice of Abel's blood represents the unceasing, collective cry of every unavenged sin, every unresolved iniquity, and every unrighteous act committed throughout the entire tragic history of humanity. It is the cumulative testimony of the fallen human condition. It is the voice that accuses the human race before a holy God, day and night (Revelation 12:10). This is the voice of the **Old Covenant of law**, which, as Paul tells us, brings condemnation, for "the letter kills" (2 Corinthians 3:6, 9). It knows nothing of grace. It only knows the balanced scales of justice.

Most critically for our study, this is the **voice of the old, Adamic bloodline.** This is the testimony carried in the veins of every son and daughter of Adam. It consistently testifies to guilt, to shame, to the deserved penalty of sin, and to the curse that is the rightful inheritance of a rebellious race. This voice is what empowers generational curses. For when the sins of the fathers—the idolatry, the violence, the covenants with darkness—go unatoned for, they create a legal demand for justice. Abel's blood cries out from the ground of your generational past, saying, "Justice has not been served! The debt has not been paid! The curse is still in effect!" It points to the sins of your forefathers and demands that the penalty be exacted from you, their children. It is the prosecuting attorney in the divine court, presenting the blood of your ancestors as Exhibit A, proving your guilt by association and your condemnation by inheritance. This voice, until silenced, holds the entire human race in a prison of deserved judgment, and it is the foundational legal basis for every generational stronghold we have discussed.

9.2 The Cry of Jesus's Blood: The Voice of the New Covenant

If the voice of Abel's blood casts the long, dark shadow of condemnation over all humanity, then the voice of Jesus's blood is the brilliant, dawn-breaking light of redemption that shatters that shadow forever. The writer of Hebrews, under the divine unction of the Holy Spirit, presents the glorious, eternal antithesis that is the believer's only hope and sure foundation. He declares to the weary, the accused, and the generationally-bound: **"You have come... to Jesus, the mediator of a new**

covenant, and to the sprinkled blood that speaks a better word than the blood of Abel." (Hebrews 12:24).

Let this truth break over your spirit like a tidal wave of grace. The blood of Jesus Christ also speaks. It is not silent. It is a witness. But its voice, its testimony, its very essence, is fundamentally and eternally different from the cry that rose from the ground east of Eden.

The blood of Abel cried from *below*, from the *ground*, from the dust of a cursed earth, and its message was "Vengeance!" But the blood of Jesus speaks from *above*, from the highest heaven, from the very **Mercy Seat** of God Himself. The book of Hebrews meticulously details this glorious transition: **"But when Christ appeared as a high priest of the good things that have come, then through the greater and more perfect tent (not made with hands, that is, not of this creation) he entered once for all into the holy places, not by means of the blood of goats and calves but by means of his own blood, thus securing an eternal redemption."** (Hebrews 9:11-12). And again, **"For Christ has entered, not into holy places made with hands, which are copies of the true things, but into heaven itself, now to appear in the presence of God on our behalf."** (Hebrews 9:24). His blood was not spilled onto the earth to be absorbed by the dust; it was presented in the heavenly tabernacle as the final, perfect, and eternally sufficient sacrifice.

And what is the content of this heavenly blood's testimony? What word does it speak from the throne of grace? It cries, **"Forgiveness! Peace! Mercy! Reconciliation! Redemption!"** It does not recite a list of your sins or the iniquities of your fathers. It bears witness not to our unrighteousness, but to **God's righteousness** and the finished work of Calvary. As Paul triumphantly declares in Romans 3:23-25, "...for all have sinned and fall short of the glory of God, and are justified by his grace as a gift, through the redemption that is in Christ Jesus, whom God put forward as a propitiation by his blood, to be received by faith. This was to show God's righteousness, because in his divine forbearance he had passed over former sins." The blood of Jesus is the public demonstration, the divine proof, that God is both just *and* the justifier of the one who has faith in Jesus (Romans 3:26).

This is why it is a **"better word."** The Greek word is *kreitton*—stronger, more excellent, more dominant, of greater weight and authority. The blood of Abel could only *demand* justice, pointing an accusing finger at the guilty. The blood of Jesus *satisfies* that very demand for justice, not by punishing the guilty, but by punishing the sin in the person of the sinless Substitute. It answers the cry of Abel's blood with a divine, "It is finished!" (John 19:30). The legal claim has been met. The debt has been paid in full. The scales of justice are perfectly balanced, not by your suffering, but by His.

Therefore, for all who are in Christ Jesus, the voice of Jesus's blood **silences the voice of Abel's blood.** When the enemy, the accuser of the brethren, stands before God and plays the recording of your father's sin, of your grandfather's failure, of the bloodline's cry for judgment, you do not need to plead your own innocence. You point to the Cross. You present the blood of Jesus. You declare, "I appeal to a higher court! I present a better witness! The blood of Jesus speaks a better word! That old testimony is null and void! The case is dismissed! The curse is broken!" The blood of Christ does not ask for mercy; it *is* mercy. It does not beg for justice; it *satisfied* justice. It is the final, eternal, and only word on your life and your lineage.

9.3 The Purity of the Witness

Beloved, to fully apprehend the cosmic authority of the "better word," we must drill down into the most fundamental distinction between these two bloods—a distinction that is not merely moral or judicial, but *ontological.* The ultimate difference lies in the **inherent purity and essential nature of the witness itself.** The voice of the blood derives its authority and the content of its testimony from the fundamental quality of the life that animates it. This is the bedrock upon which the entire legal transaction of the Cross rests.

The blood of Abel, while righteous in the sense that he was a righteous man whose sacrifice was accepted by God (Hebrews 11:4), and whom Jesus Himself called "righteous" (Matthew 23:35), was nonetheless the blood of a *fallen son of Adam.* This is a non-negotiable, sobering reality. Abel, for all his personal faith and virtue, was conceived in the natural, human way. He inherited the genetic code and the spiritual DNA of his father, Adam. The very blood that coursed through his veins, therefore, carried the inherent taint, the fatal flaw, of the original sin nature. It was blood that was part of the corrupted stream of humanity, a stream that God would later declare, "The life of the flesh is in the blood" (Leviticus 17:11), and which, because of the fall, now carried the "life" of a fallen, spiritually dead race. Abel's blood could testify to a specific, righteous act of worship, and it could cry out for justice against a specific, unrighteous act of murder. But it could not speak a word of ultimate redemption or fundamental cleansing because it was itself part of the problem. Its voice, though legitimate in its demand for justice, was the voice of a creation groaning under the curse, a voice from within the prison of sin, demanding that the rules of the prison be enforced. It was a pure testimony *about* a crime, but it was not a pure substance capable of remedying the criminal nature itself.

Now, behold the blood of Jesus! Here we encounter a hematological miracle, a biological and spiritual singularity in human history. Jesus's blood was not the blood of a man, born of a human father. He was, as the angel declared, "conceived by the Holy Spirit" (Matthew 1:20). The life-principle, the very genetic origin of His humanity, was not the seed of a fallen Adam, but the creative, life-giving power of the Spirit of God Himself. The ancient prophecy was fulfilled in its most literal sense: "The seed of the woman" would crush the serpent's head (Genesis 3:15). There was no seed of a man. Therefore, the blood that formed in the womb of the Virgin Mary was **sinless, untainted, and divine.** It carried no record of Adam's rebellion. It had no predisposition to sin. It was not a witness to the fall; it was the very life of God Himself, as Paul declared to the Ephesian elders, "...the church of God, which he obtained with his own blood." (Acts 20:28). The life in that blood was the uncreated, eternal life of the Second Person of the Godhead.

This absolute, ontological purity is what gives the voice of Jesus's blood its unparalleled, uncontestable authority. The "better word" is not just a different message—a more gracious sentiment—spoken from the same level. It is a qualitatively different message from a qualitatively different source. Abel's blood spoke from the created, fallen realm. Jesus's blood speaks from the uncreated, divine realm. It is the voice of the Creator speaking into His creation, not from the outside, but from the inside, having taken on flesh yet without its corruption. This is why His blood doesn't just *ask* for mercy; it *is* the embodiment of mercy presented before the throne. It doesn't just *request* forgiveness; it *enacts* forgiveness as a divine act. It doesn't just plead for the curse to be lifted; it *becomes* the curse (Galatians 3:13), absorbing its full force and exhausting its power, thereby silencing its voice forever.

The purity of the witness means that when you plead the blood of Jesus over your life and your bloodline, you are not applying a spiritual concept or a religious metaphor. You are invoking the supreme, court-overruling testimony of the only perfectly pure substance in the universe—the very life of God. You are bringing the witness of a sinless, divine life to bear upon the sin-stained record of your Adamic inheritance. The purity of His blood is so absolute, its authority so final, that it scours clean the ledger of generational iniquity, not by wiping the ink away, but by superimposing over it a new, perfect, and eternally valid record written in the indelible, life-giving blood of the Lamb. The voice of your fallen father's blood is drowned out by the roaring testimony of the blood of your eternal Father. This is the foundation of your freedom. This is the source of your deliverance.

9.4 Practical Application in Breaking Curses

Beloved, we have traversed the high ground of profound typology and heavenly courtroom drama. But this is not an abstract theological exercise to be filed away in a seminary library. For the believer who is weary, for the child of God who feels the weight of a generational curse—that recurring pattern of failure, that spirit of sickness, that cycle of debt—this truth is the very ground upon which you will stand to receive your deliverance. This typology provides the unshakable **judicial basis** for your freedom. It is the legal precedent that overrules every accusation from hell and nullifies every curse from your past.

Understand the enemy's primary legal strategy. He stands as the accuser of the brethren (Revelation 12:10), and his most potent evidence is the **cry of Abel's blood** emanating from your own bloodline. He presents the sins of your forefathers before the court of heaven. He points to the idolatry of your great-grandfather, the covenants with darkness made by your ancestors, the iniquities that have never been atoned for. He argues, "According to Your own law in Exodus 20:5, the iniquity of the fathers is to be visited upon the children! This curse is legally binding! This person is defined by this bloodline and deserves its judgment!" His case, based on the Old Covenant of law, is strong. The evidence seems irrefutable.

But now, you, the believer, armed with this revelation, do not respond with shame, fear, or by pleading for mercy based on your own merits. You do not try to argue that the sins of your fathers are not that bad, or that you personally are trying hard enough. Such defenses are futile against the strict letter of the law. Instead, you take your stand as a blood-bought saint. You point to an event that has forever changed the legal landscape of the universe: **the Cross of Calvary.**

You declare with holy boldness: "I acknowledge the evidence presented. But I present a superior witness. The blood of Jesus Christ speaks a **better word** than the blood of Abel. The blood of Abel cried for vengeance, but the blood of Jesus cries 'Forgiveness!' The blood of Abel demanded justice, but the blood of Jesus *satisfied* justice. The legal demand that empowered this curse has been fully met, not in me, but in the sinless Substitute, Jesus Christ. He became a curse for me, redeeming me from the curse of the law (Galatians 3:13). Therefore, this generational curse has lost its legal standing. The case is dismissed on the grounds of a higher law—the law of the Spirit of life in Christ Jesus (Romans 8:2)."

Do you see the monumental shift? You are not in the position of a beggar pleading for a pardon. You are in the position of an acquitted defendant, standing on a finished work. You are not asking for justice to be set aside; you are declaring that justice has already been perfectly served upon Christ. The curse is not merely ignored; it is legally invalidated because the condition for its power—unatoned sin demanding punishment—has been eternally satisfied.

This is how you silence the voice of the old bloodline. You do not silence it by shouting it down with positive confessions. You silence it by presenting a **superior, court-recognized testimony.** The voice of the Lamb's blood, speaking from the mercy seat in heaven, has more authority than the voice of your ancestral blood crying from the ground. When you consciously, audibly, and by faith apply the blood of Jesus to your life, to your mind, to your body, and to your generational line, you are engaging in a spiritual legal transaction. You are flooding the courtroom with a testimony that overrules all others. You are submitting the divine evidence that severs the legal claim of the enemy.

This is the practical outworking of your deliverance. When you feel the pull of a generational sin, you declare, "The blood of Jesus speaks a better word over me than the voice of this addiction." When a familiar sickness tries to manifest, you decree, "The blood of Jesus testifies to my healing, silencing the testimony of infirmity in my bloodline." When a spirit of poverty attacks, you proclaim, "The blood of Jesus cries 'Provision!' and overrules the curse of lack." You are not denying the reality of the struggle; you are enforcing a higher reality—the finished work of the Cross. You are bringing the eternal victory of Calvary into the temporal battles of your life. This is your inheritance. This is your authority. This is your freedom.

CHAPTER 10

The Paradigm of Abraham: Exiting the Father's House

Beloved, we now turn from the heavenly courtroom to the earthly pathway of deliverance. The glorious legal victory won by the blood of Christ must be walked out in our lives through deliberate acts of faith and obedience. For this, God in His wisdom has provided a supreme biblical paradigm, a living blueprint for how a "child of Destiny" breaks free from the spiritual confines of a cursed bloodline. This paradigm is the divine call of Abram, later named Abraham, recorded in Genesis 12:1. His journey is not merely ancient history; it is a prophetic template, a detailed map for your own exodus from the "house of bondage" that your generational lineage may represent.

10.1 The Threefold Command: A Progressive Separation

The Lord said to Abram, **"Go from your country and your kindred and your father's house to the land that I will show you."** (Genesis 12:1, ESV).

We must not rush past the divine precision of this command. This is not a redundant or generalized instruction to "move away." It is a meticulously structured, threefold command that delineates three concentric circles of influence, each one moving closer to the core of Abram's identity, and each one requiring a deeper, more profound level of spiritual and, in his case, physical disconnection. This is God's prescribed pattern for disentangling a human destiny from the demonic entanglements of its past.

First, "Go from your country..." This is the outermost circle of influence—the **Geographical and Cultural Context**. Your "country" represents the national spirit, the regional strongholds, the collective mindset, and the cultural idolatry of the place where you were born and raised. In Abram's case, this was Ur of the Chaldeans, a center for the worship of the moon god Nanna (or Sin). The very air he breathed was thick with a spirit of idolatry. This circle can limit a destiny by its low spiritual ceilings, its pervasive unbelief, and its systemic sins that pressure conformity. One can be bound not by a personal sin, but simply by being immersed in a spiritual environment that is hostile to God's purposes. The command to leave one's country is a call to break agreement with the territorial spirits that govern a geographical area, spirits that can assign a specific, limited destiny to everyone born under their domain.

Second, "...and your kindred..." This is the second, more intimate circle—the **Network of Extended Family and Clan**. The Hebrew word for "kindred" here is *mishpachah*, which means family, clan, or tribe. This represents the social and relational pressures, the expectations, the shared mental strongholds, and the collective behaviors of your extended family system. These are the aunts, uncles, cousins, and broader familial connections whose opinions, traditions, and shared dysfunctions can create a powerful, soulish pull away from God's unique path. It is the voice of the clan saying, "This is how we've always done things," or "No one in our family becomes that," or "You're getting too big for your britches." This circle enforces conformity through relational pressure, guilt, and the fear of being ostracized. To leave one's kindred is to be willing to stand alone, to break the power of groupthink, and to renounce the limited identity assigned by one's extended lineage.

Third, "...and your father's house." This is the innermost and most potent circle—the **Core Bloodline Inheritance**. This phrase signifies infinitely more than a physical dwelling. It represents the very core of spiritual and genetic identity, the foundational inheritance passed down through the direct paternal line. It is the "spiritual DNA." It contains the specific covenants, the pronounced blessings or curses, the core iniquities, and the defining soul wounds that are transmitted from father to child. As we have previously established, Abram's father, Terah, was an idolater (Joshua 24:2). His "house" was a house of idolatry. It was a spiritual ecosystem where false gods were served, where covenants with demons were in place, and where a limited, pagan identity was imposed. The "father's house" is the source of the most deep-seated generational patterns and curses. It is the place where the blood's testimony is most powerfully spoken and enforced. It defines who you are at the most fundamental level, or at least, who the enemy says you are.

This threefold command reveals a critical spiritual truth: **deliverance is a progressive separation.** God does not typically deliver us from all our chains at once. He leads us out in stages, dealing first with the external environments, then with the relational networks, and finally with the core identity-level strongholds. Many believers try to deal with the core curses while still fully immersed in the "country" and "kindred" that reinforce them, and they wonder why their progress is so slow and difficult. God's pattern for Abraham, and for you, is a deliberate, step-by-step exodus from every level of influence that contradicts His divine purpose for your life.

10.2 The Critical Distinction: Leaving Country vs. Leaving Father's House

We now arrive at what is perhaps the most pivotal and misunderstood revelation in this entire paradigm. There exists a profound, even terrifying, mystery in God's threefold command: **one can successfully and completely obey the first two commands—leaving country and kindred—while remaining utterly and completely imprisoned within the third and most critical sphere: the "father's house."** This distinction is the difference between a geographical relocation and a generational revolution, between a change of scenery and a change of destiny.

Let us be brutally practical. An individual can physically emigrate from South Africa to the United Kingdom. They can leave behind the specific territorial spirits, the national strongholds, and the cultural limitations of their native land. They can also, with determined effort, distance themselves from their "kindred"—the extended family, the demanding relatives, the negative social circle back home. They can build a new life in a new nation, with new friends and a new address. By all outward appearances, they have obeyed God's command. They have "gone out."

Yet, in this new nation, under this new sky, they may find themselves besieged by the *exact same demons* that tormented their lineage for generations. The spirit of poverty that haunted their grandfather in a rural village may now manifest as a series of inexplicable financial collapses in the heart of London. The familial curse of diabetes or heart disease that plagued their parents may now be diagnosed in their own body, despite a change in diet and environment. The relational patterns of divorce, betrayal, or loneliness that defined their family tree may now replay themselves in their new relationships in this new culture. They have changed their location, their passport, and their social network, but they have not changed their **spiritual inheritance.** They are in a new country, but they are still living, breathing, and struggling within the spiritual confines of Terah's house. They brought the prison with them.

This is because the "father's house" is not a physical location; it is a **spiritual and soulish reality carried within the individual.** It is the internalized record of the bloodline, the core identity shaped by ancestral covenants and iniquities. It is the "ancient boundary stone" set by your forefathers (Proverbs 22:28), which defines the borders of your life. You can travel to the other side of the world, but you cannot outrun the witness in your own blood. The strongholds of the "father's house" are embedded in the very fabric of your soul and spirit—in your thought patterns, your emotional responses, your unconscious beliefs, and your deepest fears. They are the "familiar spirits" that are familiar with *you*, not with your zip code.

This is why so many believers experience frustration in their walk with God. They have physically and socially separated from toxic environments, they are serving in church, reading the Bible, and praying fervently, yet they cannot seem to break through certain persistent cycles. They are trying to build the future of Abraham while still carrying the core identity of Terah. They have left Ur, but they have not left the house of their father. The spiritual legalities of that house—the curses, the assignments, the familiar spirits—still have jurisdiction because they have never been explicitly renounced and broken by the superior authority of the blood of Jesus and the power of the Holy Spirit.

The call to leave the "father's house" is therefore primarily an *internal, spiritual, and judicial* command. It is a call to sever the spiritual umbilical cord that connects you to the sinful patterns, curses, and false identities of your paternal lineage. It is a conscious, faith-filled act of disinheriting yourself from the kingdom of darkness and fully claiming your new inheritance in Christ. It is the recognition that your true Father is God Himself, and your true "house" is the household of faith (Ephesians 2:19), built upon the foundation of the apostles and prophets, with Christ Jesus Himself as the chief cornerstone. Until this internal exodus is complete, no amount of external change can produce lasting freedom. The battle is not against geography or genetics, but against the spiritual powers that have used those things to build a fortress around your destiny.

10.3 The Result of Obedience: A New Identity and Legacy

The radical obedience of Abram to this threefold command was not merely the first step in his journey; it was the non-negotiable prerequisite that unlocked the entirety of his divine destiny and the generational blessings that would flow from it. The profound theological principle established here is this: **God could not fully bless Abram, could not pour out the fullness of His covenant promise, while Abram was still definitionally and spiritually connected to an idolatrous system.** The blessing and the curse could not coexist in the same spiritual space. The new wine of God's promise required new wineskins, and the old wineskin of Terah's house had to be decisively left behind.

The magnificent blessing of Genesis 12:2-3 was explicitly contingent upon his exit: **"I will make of you a great nation, and I will bless you and make your name great, so that you will be a blessing. I will bless those who bless you, and him who dishonors you I will curse, and in you all the families of the earth shall be blessed."** This promise—of nationhood, of personal blessing, of a great name, of divine protection, and of global redemptive influence—was not activated the moment God spoke it. It was activated the moment Abram *obeyed* and severed the ties that bound him to the system that contradicted it. His physical departure from Haran was the outward sign of an inward severance. By leaving, Abram was not just changing his address; he was performing a prophetic act, a spiritual surgery that cut the umbilical cord connecting him to a destiny of idolatry, obscurity, and irrelevance. He was disconnecting from the spiritual power grid of his father's house and plugging into the limitless generator of God's covenant promise.

The dramatic contrast in outcomes proves this point with stark, historical finality. Abram had two biological brothers: Nahor and Haran (Genesis 11:26-27). They remained in Mesopotamia, within the geographical, social, and spiritual sphere of their father Terah's house. And what became of them? They faded into utter historical and spiritual irrelevance. They are mere footnotes in the genealogical record, their names preserved only as they relate to the story of Abram. They were consumed by the spiritual atmosphere they chose to remain in. Their legacy was limited, their destiny defined by the pagan context of Ur and Haran.

Abram, however, the one who dared to obey, the one who exited the old system, became the father of faith (Romans 4:16), the friend of God (James 2:23), and the patriarch of nations. His name was changed from Abram ("Exalted Father") to Abraham ("Father of a Multitude") as a seal of his new identity (Genesis 17:5). His legacy was not one of obscure idolatry but of global redemption, for it is through his "seed," who is Christ (Galatians 3:16), that all the families of the earth are indeed blessed. The obedience of one man to exit a cursed spiritual inheritance resulted in an eternal legacy of blessing for all humanity.

This is the potent promise held out to every "child of Destiny" today. Your obedience to spiritually "exit your father's house"—to renounce its curses, to break its covenants, to reject its false identities—is the very key that unlocks your promised land. It is the decisive act that allows God to fully release the blessing that has your name on it. You cannot cling to the security of the familiar, fallen identity and simultaneously lay hold of the limitless identity God has for you in Christ. You must choose. Will you remain in the house of Terah, with its defined but limited boundaries, or will you, like Abraham, step out in obedient faith into the unknown, trusting that the God who calls you is also the God who will redefine you, re-identity you, and establish a legacy through you that will shake the nations for His glory? The blessing is contingent upon the exit. Your new name and your new legacy await on the other side of your obedience.

10.4 New Testament Application: The Call to Discipleship

The Abrahamic paradigm, etched in the early chapters of Genesis, is not an isolated historical account. It is the foundational archetype, the divine prototype, that finds its ultimate fulfillment and universal application in the radical call of the Lord Jesus Christ. The command to leave "country, kindred, and father's house" is transposed into a higher, more profound key in the New Covenant, becoming the non-negotiable entry point into authentic discipleship. The geographical and familial separation required of Abraham becomes, for the believer in Christ, a spiritual and ontological separation from the entire Adamic order.

Jesus declared with unsettling clarity: **"If anyone comes to me and does not hate his own father and mother and wife and children and brothers and sisters, yes, and even his own life, he cannot be my disciple."** (Luke 14:26, ESV). We must understand this statement within its Hebraic context. This is not a command to cultivate emotional animosity or to neglect God-given familial responsibilities (a command He elsewhere upholds, see Matthew 15:4-6). This is the use of drastic, hyperbolic language—a rabbinic idiom—to establish a fundamental principle of **absolute priority and comparative devotion.** The call to "hate" one's family in this context means to love them less by comparison, to renounce any claim they have that would rival the supreme allegiance demanded by Christ. It is the conscious, deliberate dethroning of every natural and spiritual tie from the central place of influence in one's life.

This is the New Testament equivalent of leaving the "father's house." The "father" in this context is not merely one's biological parent, but the entire Adamic lineage, the "father of lies" (John 8:44) who stands behind the cursed inheritance of the fallen race. The "house" is the kingdom of darkness, the spiritual ecosystem of sin, death, and the curse, into which every human is born. To be a disciple of Jesus is to answer the call to spiritually and decisively exit that house. It is to renounce the identity, the inheritance, and the legal claims of that old Adamic bloodline, just as Abraham renounced the house of Terah.

This is why the Apostle Paul can declare the breathtaking truth: **"He has delivered us from the domain of darkness and transferred us to the kingdom of his beloved Son,"** (Colossians 1:13, ESV). The Greek word for "transferred" is *methistēmi*, meaning to transpose, to remove from one place to another, to change a thing's situation. This is the New Covenant exodus! This is the spiritual reality that corresponds to Abraham's physical journey. Your discipleship began with a sovereign act of God, transferring you out of the spiritual "country" of darkness. But you must now walk out that reality by daily "hating"—by renouncing, rejecting, and disinheriting—the lingering influences, patterns, and identities of that former domain, including those that flow through your natural family lines.

To follow Christ, therefore, is to embark on the same journey as Abraham. It is to leave behind:

- The "country" of the world's value system and godless culture (Romans 12:2).
- The "kindred" of ungodly soul ties and relationships that pull you away from destiny (2 Corinthians 6:14-18).
- The "father's house" of the old, sinful nature and its generational curses, embracing instead your new

identity as a son or daughter of God, a member of the household of faith (Ephesians 2:19).

Abraham's journey is the archetype. He is the father of all who believe (Romans 4:11), and his pattern of exit and obedience is the pattern for every one of his spiritual children. You cannot cling to the security of your Adamic inheritance and its associated curses while trying to claim your inheritance in Christ. The call to discipleship is a call to a clean break, a decisive exit, and a wholehearted embrace of a new Father, a new family, a new citizenship, and a new, eternal legacy.

CHAPTER 11

The Zion Reality: Our Position in Christ

Beloved, we have journeyed through the legal foundations, the typological contrasts, and the practical paradigms of breaking free from generational curses. Now we arrive at the glorious culmination, the ultimate reality that makes all our deliverance not just a defensive battle but a triumphant occupation of our God-given territory. The Abrahamic paradigm of exiting the old "father's house" finds its ultimate and eternal fulfillment not in a geographical location in the Middle East, but in a profound and present spiritual reality: **Mount Zion.** The New Testament reveals with stunning clarity that the believer's deliverance from the old Adamic bloodline is not merely a matter of breaking curses one by one, as vital as that is, but of having been decisively **translated into a new kingdom where curses have no legal jurisdiction.** Our freedom is not just the absence of a chain; it is the presence of a crown. It is not just an escape from Egypt; it is an enthronement in Zion.

11.1 The City Abraham Sought

We must understand that Abraham's obedience was fueled by a vision that stretched far beyond the horizons of Canaan. His eyes were fixed on a reality that made the temporal promises of land and descendants into mere signposts pointing to a greater, eternal inheritance. The writer of Hebrews unveils the true object of Abraham's faith: **"For he was looking forward to the city that has foundations, whose designer and builder is God."** (Hebrews 11:10, ESV).

The text does not say he was looking forward to *Canaan*. It says he was looking forward to a *city*. This is a seismic shift in understanding. The land of promise, flowing with milk and honey, was never the ultimate destination. It was a type, a shadow, a divine metaphor for a permanent, unshakable reality. Abraham understood that the earthly Canaan was a provisional fulfillment, a down payment on a cosmic inheritance. The tents in which he and Isaac and Jacob dwelt as "strangers and exiles on the earth" (Hebrews 11:13) were a conscious testimony that their true citizenship was elsewhere. They were "looking forward," (the Greek *ekdechomai* means to await eagerly, to expect) to something that God Himself had architected and constructed.

This city is distinguished by its "foundations." Every human city is built on temporary, shifting foundations—economic systems, political power, cultural trends, all of which are subject to decay and collapse. But the city Abraham sought has eternal, unshakable foundations—the very righteousness, justice, and covenant faithfulness of God. Its designer (*technitēs*—architect, craftsman) and builder (*dēmiourgos*—creator, artisan) is God. This means its origin is divine, its blueprint is perfect, and its construction is guaranteed. It is the anti-Babel. At Babel, humanity sought to "make a name for ourselves" (Genesis 11:4) by building a city to reach heaven. Here, God builds a city and brings it down to those who, like Abraham, trust in His name.

This forward-looking faith of Abraham reframes his entire journey. His exodus from Ur was not merely a departure *from* an idolatrous house, but a pilgrimage *toward* a divine city. His obedience was not rooted in rejection alone, but in a powerful, magnetic attraction to a superior inheritance. He left the house of Terah because he had seen the blueprint of a house built by God. This is the ultimate motivation for our own exodus from the old, cursed bloodline. It is not enough to simply hate our bondage; we must be captivated by a vision of our freedom. We are not just fleeing the house of slavery; we are marching toward the City of God. Our deliverance is purposeful; it is our journey to Zion.

11.2 The Believer's Present Position

The narrative of faith shifts dramatically with the inauguration of the New Covenant. What was for Abraham and the patriarchs a distant vision, a future hope to be eagerly anticipated through a lifetime of pilgrimage, has become for the believer in Christ a present-tense, possessed reality. The staggering, almost incomprehensible revelation of the New Covenant is this: **we do not have to embark on a lifelong journey to find this city, for we have already arrived.** The pilgrimage is over; the occupation has begun.

The writer of Hebrews makes this declaration with theological precision that should cause every believer to rise to their feet in triumphant praise: **"But you have come to Mount Zion and to the city of the living God, the heavenly Jerusalem..."** (Hebrews 12:22, ESV). Let us dissect this declaration with the reverence it demands. The Greek verb translated "have come" is *proselēlythate* (προσεληλύθατε). This is not a future tense, nor is it a present tense describing a continuous process. It is in the **perfect tense**, one of the most significant grammatical features in the Greek New Testament. The perfect tense describes a completed action in the past that has results and effects that continue into the present. It is a state of being. It signifies a finished, settled, and abiding reality.

This means that your position in Zion is not something you are striving toward, praying for, or hoping to attain upon death. It is a *fait accompli*—a done deal. By virtue of the new birth, through your union with Christ in His death and resurrection, you have been spiritually and legally transferred. This is the explicit testimony of Colossians 1:13: **"He has delivered us from the domain of darkness and transferred us to the kingdom of his beloved Son."** The Greek word for "transferred" here is *methistēmi*, a powerful term used for the relocation of entire populations or the moving of goods from one warehouse to another. It is a decisive, sovereign act of the King. You are not a tourist visiting Zion; you are a naturalized citizen, with all the rights, privileges, and immunities thereof. Your spiritual GPS has been permanently reprogrammed. You are no longer located in the "domain of darkness," which includes the jurisdiction of every generational curse; you are now, and forever, located "in Christ," who is seated in the heavenly places at the right hand of the Father (Ephesians 2:6).

This is the ultimate foundation for your freedom from generational curses. A curse is a legal instrument that operates within a specific jurisdiction—the kingdom of darkness, the "father's house" of Adam. But you are no longer in that jurisdiction! You have been given a new legal residence. When the enemy, the accuser, brings a charge against you based on the sins of your forefathers, he is filing a lawsuit in the wrong court. You can stand in the authority of your new citizenship and declare, "I am no longer subject to the laws of that old kingdom. I am in Christ, in Zion. The blood of Jesus has silenced the witness of my old bloodline. This court has no jurisdiction over me." Your position in Zion is your ultimate legal defense. It is the unassailable, high ground from which you enforce the victory of the Cross over every echo of the curse in your life. You are not fighting *for* victory; you are fighting *from* victory. You are not trying to get *into* Zion; you are commanding the forces of darkness to leave the territory of Zion, which is your life, your mind, your body, and your destiny.

11.3 The Legal Environment of Zion

Beloved, understanding our positional transfer to Zion is the foundational truth, but to wield this truth as a weapon against generational curses, we must comprehend the **legal environment** of this kingdom into which we have been translated. A kingdom's power is expressed through its laws, its decrees, and the rights it grants its citizens. The jurisdiction of Zion is not a passive location; it is a dynamic realm governed by divine statutes that directly contradict and nullify the laws of the kingdom of darkness. The power of this truth to shatter bloodline curses lies in the absolute dominion and immunity that characterize this environment.

The prophet Isaiah, peering through the veil of time, was given a breathtaking glimpse of the legal atmosphere of Zion. He declares a decree that should resonate in the spirit of every believer battling generational strongholds: **"And no inhabitant will say, 'I am sick'; the people who dwell there will be forgiven their iniquity."** (Isaiah 33:24, ESV). This is not merely a poetic description of a future heaven; it is a prophetic declaration of the present-tense legal reality for everyone who is "in Christ," the true Zion. Let us break down this foundational statute.

First, "No inhabitant will say, 'I am sick'..." This establishes a legal precedent concerning **physical health**. In the jurisdiction of Zion, sickness has no legal right to establish a permanent residence or define the identity of a citizen. The generational patterns of disease and infirmity that travel down family lines—the diabetes, the cancers, the heart conditions, the autoimmune disorders—derive their legal power from the curse of the law and the testimony of the old bloodline. But in Zion, that legal ground has been revoked. The believer who is awakened to this reality does not practice a form of "name-it-and-claim-it" denial of symptoms. Rather, they engage in a judicial process. When a symptom of a generational illness manifests, they do not receive it as their identity or their inevitable portion. Instead, they stand in their authority as a citizen of Zion and assert a higher legal truth. They declare, "I am an inhabitant of Zion, in Christ Jesus. The law of this kingdom states that no inhabitant says, 'I am sick.' Therefore, this symptom is an illegal alien in my body, a trespasser with no legal standing. I enforce the health and wholeness that are my covenant right in this kingdom, based on the stripes of Jesus (1 Peter 2:24)." You are not begging God to heal you; you are commanding the spirit of infirmity to leave the territory over which it has no legal authority—your body, which is the temple of the Holy Spirit, located in Zion.

Second, "...the people who dwell there will be forgiven their iniquity." This is the cornerstone of the entire legal structure. The Hebrew word for "forgiven" is *nasa*, which means to bear, to carry away, to take away. In the Greek New Testament, the word used is *aphiēmi* (ἀφίημι), which carries the powerful legal connotation of sending away, releasing from an obligation, canceling a debt, or pardoning a crime. In the jurisdiction of Zion, the iniquities of the forefathers have been *sent away*. The legal basis for every generational curse—the unatoned for, unresolved iniquity that created a debt demanding punishment upon the descendants—has been **nullified and canceled**. The blood of Jesus has not merely covered the record; it has cleansed it, expunging it from the heavenly ledger (Colossians 2:14). The enemy's primary legal brief, which he uses to enforce generational curses, is the list of ancestral sins crying out for justice. But in Zion, the Supreme Judge has declared that the debt has been paid in full by the blood of the Lamb. The case has been dismissed with prejudice. The curse has lost its legal standing because the condition that empowered it—unpunished sin—has been eternally satisfied.

Therefore, when you take your stand in Zion, you are positioning yourself in a legal environment where the most fundamental building blocks of generational curses—sickness and unforgiven iniquity—are rendered powerless. You are no longer subject to the laws of the old country. You are under a new constitution, whose foundational articles guarantee your healing and your absolute freedom from the guilt, penalty, and legal consequences of all sin—past, present, and generational. This is your legal ground for freedom. This is the authority with which you command every lingering echo of the curse to be silent and to leave.

11.4 The Communal Nature of Zion

The glorious truth of our position in Zion must never be misunderstood as a solitary, individualistic spiritual experience. One of the most devastating tactics of generational curses is the spirit of isolation they breed, convincing the individual that they are alone in their struggle, a solitary warrior facing a familial giant that no one else can understand or conquer. The enemy knows that a isolated believer is a vulnerable believer. But the revelation of Zion shatters this lie with the brilliant, overwhelming truth of our **corporate, communal identity.**

The writer of Hebrews, after declaring our arrival at Mount Zion, immediately expands the vision to reveal the teeming, triumphant community into which we have been immersed:

"But you have come to Mount Zion and to the city of the living God, the heavenly Jerusalem, and to innumerable angels in festal gathering, and to the assembly of the firstborn who are enrolled in heaven, and to God, the judge of all, and to the spirits of the righteous made perfect, and to Jesus, the mediator of a new covenant..." (Hebrews 12:22-24, ESV).

This is not a picture of a private audience with God. This is a cosmic celebration, a triumphant assembly. Let us unpack the constituents of this community, for your authority is embedded within it.

First, you have come to **"innumerable angels in festal gathering."** The Greek word for "innumerable" is *muriasin*, from which we get "myriads," meaning tens of thousands, an uncountable host. These are not passive observers; they are mighty warriors in a "festal gathering" (*panēgyris*—a public, joyous assembly for a celebration, like the Olympic games). They are mobilized, ministering spirits sent out to serve for the sake of those who are to inherit salvation (Hebrews 1:14). When you wage war against a generational curse, you are not summoning angels as a lone petitioner; you are a commanding officer in a army whose angelic ranks are already mustered and deployed. The collective power of this angelic host dwarfs any "familiar spirit" assigned to your bloodline.

Second, you have come to **"the assembly of the firstborn who are enrolled in heaven."** This is the *ekklēsia*, the church, the called-out ones. These are your brothers and sisters in Christ, the "firstborn" who share in the inheritance of the Firstborn, Jesus Himself (Romans 8:29). Their names are written in the Lamb's book of life. This is critical: you are part of a new bloodline, a new family tree. The isolated, negative testimony of your single, fallen bloodline is now overwhelmed by the combined, righteous testimony of the entire body of Christ. You are no longer just "John Doe, descendant of alcoholics and adulterers." You are "John Doe, member of the assembly of the firstborn, a citizen of Zion, a son of the Living God." The legal weight of this new corporate identity cancels the old, isolated identity. The curses that operated through the channel of your biological family cannot flow through the channel of your spiritual family, the church.

Third, you have come to **"the spirits of the righteous made perfect."** This is the great cloud of witnesses (Hebrews 12:1)—the Abrahams, the Isaacs, the Jacobs, the prophets and apostles who have finished their race. You are surrounded by the completed testimonies of those who themselves broke generational strongholds and walked in faith. Their victories stand as eternal precedents in the court of heaven, reinforcing your own legal case.

This communal reality refutes the lie of isolation absolutely. The believer is not a lone individual fighting a familial giant. You are a member of an innumerable company, a royal priesthood, a holy nation (1 Peter 2:9). When you stand in prayer to break a generational curse, you do so as part of this "general assembly." The combined authority of this body, the collective power of its testimony, and the shared victory of its Head, Jesus Christ, overpower the isolated, limited testimony of your single, fallen bloodline. You are fighting from a position of overwhelming numerical, spiritual, and legal superiority. The giant of your family curse is not facing you alone; it is facing the entire army of the living God, with the Captain of our salvation at its head. This is the Zion reality. This is your inheritance. This is your family.

CHAPTER 12

Awakening to the New Creation Reality

Beloved, we have now ascended to the summit of revealed truth. We have established our legal position in the unassailable fortress of Zion, a transfer accomplished by the sheer grace and power of God through the finished work of the Cross. Yet, a profound chasm often exists between this glorious positional truth and the daily, experiential reality of many believers. They are, in truth, legally seated in heavenly places in Christ Jesus (Ephesians 2:6), yet they live, feel, and struggle as if they are still prisoners in the desert of their former inheritance, besieged by the same generational giants. The second key to walking in sustained freedom—after understanding our position—is the critical, deliberate, and ongoing process of **awakening** to it. We must move from being citizens of Zion in doctrine to being conscious inhabitants of Zion in experience.

12.1 The "Behold" of 2 Corinthians 5:17

The Apostle Paul, under the inspiration of the Holy Spirit, delivers one of the most concentrated theological statements in all of Scripture, a verse that serves as the bedrock of our new identity: **"Therefore, if anyone is in Christ, he is a new creation. The old has passed away; behold, the new has come."** (2 Corinthians 5:17, ESV).

We must linger here, for within this single verse lies the divine mechanism for our awakening. Many can quote this scripture, yet live in contradiction to its truth. The key to its application is found in a single, potent word that is often glossed over: **"Behold!"**

The Greek word is *idou* (ἰδοὺ). This is not a filler word or a simple conjunction. It is a term of arresting attention, a divine trumpet blast, a command to stop, look, and perceive. It is used throughout Scripture to signal a dramatic, often sudden, shift in reality that requires a corresponding shift in perception. When the angel appeared to the shepherds, he said, "*Behold*, I bring you good news..." (Luke 2:10). When John the Baptist saw Jesus, he declared, "*Behold*, the Lamb of God..." (John 1:29). The word "*behold*" is a summons to awaken to a new reality that has just broken into the old one. In 2 Corinthians 5:17, God Himself is shouting, "Wake up! Pay attention! A cosmic shift has occurred! Stop looking at the old and *behold* the new!"

What are we to behold? We are to behold the fact that **"the old has passed away."** The Greek verb for "passed away" is *parerchomai* (παρέρχομαι). It means to pass away, to vanish, to perish, to become invalid, to lose its power and authority. This is a definitive statement. The "old" here is the entire Adamic existence—the old, cursed bloodline with its patterns, its cycles, its legal grounds for demonic oppression, its identity of sin and death. Its power is not merely weakened; it is broken. Its legal claim is not just challenged; it is invalidated. It has *passed away* in the same way that a canceled debt passes away from the ledger. The generational curse that once defined your family's story has lost its binding authority over you.

And what has taken its place? We are to behold that **"the new has come."** The verb here is *ginomai* (γίνομαι), meaning to come into existence, to begin to be, to happen, to become a present reality. This is not a future hope. This is a present-tense fact. The "new" is the new creation—your reborn spirit, your new identity in Christ, your citizenship in Zion, your righteous standing before God. It is not something you are becoming; it is something you *are*. "New" in Greek is *kainos* (καινός), meaning not just new in time, but new in quality, fresh, unprecedented. This new creation is a species of being that never existed before, forged in the resurrection life of Jesus Christ.

Therefore, the "behold" is the divine command to transfer your focus. You are to stop beholding the persistent echoes of the old creation—the recurring thoughts, the familiar feelings, the symptoms in your body that align with the old curse—and to steadfastly *behold* the settled reality of the new creation. You are not in denial; you are in faith. You are choosing to agree with God's "behold" over the enemy's "behold." When the enemy says, "Behold, the same sickness that was in your father!" you respond, "I behold the stripes of Jesus by which I am healed (1 Peter 2:24). I am a new creation." When he whispers, "Behold, the pattern of failure that runs in your bloodline!" you declare, "I behold the righteousness of God in Christ. I am a new creation. The old has passed away." This is the fight of faith—the fight to keep your spiritual eyes fixed on what God says is true, until that truth manifests fully in your experience.

12.2 The Dynamics of Awakening

The divine command to "behold" initiates a process, a spiritual discipline of reorientation that I term **The Dynamics of Awakening.** This is not a passive, mystical experience that overtakes us without our participation. It is the active, willful, and sustained process by which the human spirit—already perfectly renewed and one with the Lord (1 Corinthians 6:17)—and the soul (the mind, will, and emotions) progressively come into alignment with the legal truth of the new creation. It is the daily working out of our salvation with fear and trembling, knowing that it is God who works in us (Philippians 2:12-13). This awakening involves three interconnected, dynamic disciplines.

First, and foremost, is the Renewed Mind. The Apostle Paul issues a non-negotiable command in Romans 12:2: **"Do not be conformed to this world, but be transformed by the renewal of your mind, that by testing you may discern what is the will of God, what is good and acceptable and perfect."** The Greek word for "transformed" is *metamorphoō*, from which we get "metamorphosis." It signifies a complete, fundamental change of form, like a caterpillar becoming a butterfly. This transformation is not achieved by sheer willpower, but "by the renewal of your mind."

Your mind has been programmed for decades, even generations, by the old, Adamic bloodline. It has been conditioned by the lies of the enemy, spoken through family narratives, cultural expectations, and personal failures. These lies form deep neural pathways of unbelief: "I am poor," "I am sickly,"

"I am a failure," "This is just how our family is." To awaken to the new creation reality is to engage in a systematic, ruthless campaign of deprogramming and reprogramming. It is to take every thought captive to obey Christ (2 Corinthians 10:5). This means you must actively, deliberately replace the old, familiar lies with the specific, potent truth of God's Word concerning your identity in Zion. When the thought comes, "You'll never get out of debt," you must counter it with the truth: "My God supplies all my needs according to his riches in glory in Christ Jesus" (Philippians 4:19). You do this not once, but consistently, until the new, godly neural pathway is more familiar and more powerful than the old, demonic one. This is the foundational work without which all other spiritual warfare will be unstable.

Second, is the Power of Conscious Declaration. God created the universe *ex nihilo* (out of nothing) by the power of His spoken word (Genesis 1, Hebrews 11:3). He has designed reality to be shaped by authoritative speech. Of Abraham, it is said, **"in the presence of the God in whom he believed, who gives life to the dead and calls into existence the things that do not exist."** (Romans 4:17). As children of God, created in His image, we are called to operate in the same principle. Your tongue is not merely for communicating; it is a creative and enforcing weapon.

Conscious declaration is the practice of using your tongue to call those things that are not (in the natural, visible realm) as though they were (in the spiritual, legal realm). When you declare, "I am healed," while feeling symptoms, you are not lying. You are enforcing the superior legal reality of Zion over the temporary, illegal symptom in your body. You are, in a sense, "calling your body" to align with the truth of 1 Peter 2:24. When you declare, "I am prosperous," in the face of lack, you are calling your financial situation to align with the truth of 2 Corinthians 8:9. This is not positive thinking; it is prophetic enforcement. You are issuing a decree from the court of heaven, based on the finished work of the Cross, and commanding the natural realm to conform. Every declaration of "I am" that aligns with Scripture is a hammer blow to the old, false identity imposed by the generational curse.

Third, is the Discipline of Reckoning. This is a term beautifully captured in the King James Version of Romans 6:11: **"Likewise reckon ye also yourselves to be dead indeed unto sin, but alive unto God through Jesus Christ our Lord."** The Greek word for "reckon" is *logizomai*, an accounting term meaning to calculate, to take into account, to consider something as settled fact. This is not a feeling; it is a faith-based calculation.

You are commanded to "reckon" yourself dead to sin—and by extension, dead to the old, sinful bloodline and its curses. This means that when the old nature, or a familiar generational pattern, rears its head, you do not debate with it. You do not negotiate. You simply refer to the ledger of your life and declare, "According to the books of heaven, that person is dead. That identity was crucified with Christ. I am no longer in that account. I have been transferred to the 'alive unto God' account." You count it as true, regardless of the emotional or physical evidence to the contrary. You are agreeing with God's "behold." This reckoning is the bridge between the renewed mind and the powerful declaration. Your mind has been renewed by the truth, you reckon that truth as the final authority in your life, and then you declare that truth into your circumstances, commanding them to align with the reckoning. This is the dynamic process of awakening—the daily, moment-by-moment practice of enforcing your Zion reality until it becomes your lived experience.

12.3 The Testimony of the Blood in the Believer

We arrive now at the ultimate frontier of this awakening, the final and most intimate battleground where the war for your identity is won or lost. For the believer who is being progressively awakened to the reality of their new creation status in Zion, a profound and transformative shift occurs in the very witness of their physical being. **The blood in their veins is no longer the primary, authoritative witness over their life.** This is a seismic shift in spiritual hematology. Biologically, the blood may still carry the genetic code, the markers, and the physical predispositions of the Adamic lineage. But its *spiritual authority* to define, to dictate destiny, and to enforce curses has been utterly and permanently **superseded**.

The dominant, overriding testimony in the life of the awakened believer is no longer the faint, condemning echo of Abel's blood from their ancestral past. The preeminent witness is now the internal, powerful, and life-affirming voice of **the Spirit of God Himself, bearing witness with our spirit that we are children of God** (Romans 8:16). The Greek word for "bear witness with" is *summartureō*, meaning to testify together, to corroborate jointly. This is a collaborative testimony. The Holy Spirit, from His dwelling place within your reborn human spirit, constantly affirms, confirms, and declares your true sonship. He testifies to your forgiveness, your acceptance, your righteousness, and your inheritance. This internal witness becomes the loudest voice in your life, the baseline reality from which you operate.

This fundamental shift changes the entire direction of your existence. You cease to live *from the outside in*—allowing external circumstances, physical symptoms, or old familial patterns to dictate your identity and emotional state. Instead, you learn to live *from the inside out*—from your reborn spirit, which is filled with the Holy Spirit and saturated with the Word of God. Your spirit, illuminated by the Spirit and informed by the Scripture, becomes the command center. It interprets circumstances, rather than being interpreted by them. It judges symptoms, rather than being judged by them.

Therefore, when a thought, a compulsive impulse, a wave of fear, or a physical symptom arises that perfectly aligns with a known generational pattern, the awakened saint does not receive it as "who I am." They have been trained by the discipline of a renewed mind to recognize it for what it is: **an echo from a defeated kingdom.** It is a ghost, a phantom signal from a transmitter whose power has been cut. It is the last, desperate broadcast of a dethroned ruler trying to maintain control through psychological and spiritual guerrilla warfare.

The response of the awakened believer is immediate, authoritative, and rooted in their legal standing. They do not ignore the echo; they confront it with the superior word. They declare, with the full authority of their citizenship in Zion:

- **"I am in Christ. That is not my portion."**
- **"I am the righteousness of God in Him (2 Corinthians 5:21). That accusation of guilt and failure has no legal standing."**
- **"That sickness has no legal right to me. By His stripes, I was healed (1 Peter 2:24)."**

- **"That spirit of poverty has no legal right to me. For I know the grace of my Lord Jesus Christ, that though he was rich, yet for my sake he became poor, so that I by his poverty might become rich (2 Corinthians 8:9)."**
- **"My life is hidden with Christ in God (Colossians 3:3). You are attacking a shadow; the substance of my life is safe in the unassailable fortress of the Godhead."**

This, beloved, is the practical, moment-by-moment outworking of breaking bloodline curses. It is not a one-time prayer that magically erases all future struggle. It is the daily, conscious, and willful **enforcement of the victory of the Cross** through a conscious, awakened identity. It is the lived experience of what it means to "work out your own salvation" (Philippians 2:12)—to manifest in the external realm what is already true in the internal, spiritual realm. You are pulling down the strongholds of the past by relentlessly affirming the superior reality of your present position in Christ. You are, quite literally, living your way into your freedom, one faithful declaration, one renewed thought, one act of reckoning at a time. The old blood may speak, but its voice is now a whisper drowned out by the roaring testimony of the Spirit and the Word. You are no longer a prisoner of your heredity; you are a pioneer of your destiny in Christ.

CHAPTER 13

The Ministry of Deliverance: Addressing Attachment and Attack

Beloved, we have now established the impregnable legal fortress of our position in Christ. We are seated in Zion, new creations, our old identity crucified and our bloodline redeemed by the superior testimony of the Lamb's blood. Yet, we must be ruthlessly practical. The outworking of this glorious legal reality in our daily experience often requires us to engage in the **ministry of deliverance.** Just because a squatter's lease has been legally invalidated does not mean he will leave the property without being confronted and evicted. A mature, biblically sound understanding recognizes that not all spiritual oppression is the same. Precise diagnosis is critical for effective ministry, lest we use a scalpel where a sword is needed, or offer spiritual aspirin for a condition that requires major surgery. We must carefully distinguish between the related but distinct states of oppression: **possession, attachment, and attack.**

13.1 The Spectrum of Oppression

The popular imagination, often shaped more by Hollywood than by the Holy Word, tends to envision demonic activity in its most extreme and dramatic form. However, Scripture and extensive pastoral and deliverance ministry reveal a nuanced spectrum of oppression. Failing to discern these distinctions can lead to misdirected ministry, causing us to cast out demons that are not there, or to overlook subtle strongholds that are wreaking havoc in a believer's life.

First, on the extreme end of the spectrum, is Demon Possession.

This term, derived from the Greek *daimonizomai* (which simply means "to be demonized"), describes a state where a demonic entity or legion has gained such a profound degree of internal control over an individual's faculties that it can speak through them, manipulate their body, and direct their actions against their own will. The classic biblical example is the Gerasene demoniac of Mark 5:1-20. This man lived among the tombs, could not be bound with chains, cried out night and day, and cut himself with stones. The demons within him spoke directly to Jesus, acknowledging His identity and begging for mercy. This represents the ultimate internal takeover, where the person's soul and body have become a vessel occupied and operated by a hostile spiritual force. It is crucial to understand that this extreme state is **typically, if not exclusively, found in those with no covenant relationship with Jesus Christ.** A believer, whose spirit is the temple of the Holy Spirit (1 Corinthians 6:19), cannot be "possessed" in this ultimate sense, for God and demons cannot co-habitate the same core sanctuary. However, the outer courts of the soul and body can be profoundly influenced, which leads us to the next category.

Second, and far more common among believers, is Spirit Attachment.

This is a state where a demonic spirit is not in control of the person's core, reborn identity (their spirit, which is one with the Lord, 1 Corinthians 6:17), but it has formed an *attachment* to a specific, unhealed, or compromised area of their soul or body. This attachment is often facilitated by a legal ground, such as:

- A **generational iniquity** that has not been renounced and cleansed by the blood of Jesus, providing a familiar, "welcome" environment for a specific type of spirit (e.g., a spirit of addiction attached to a bloodline history of alcoholism).
- A **deep soul wound** or trauma, such as severe rejection, abuse, or betrayal, that creates an entry point for a spirit of fear, shame, or bitterness.
- A **persistent, unrepentant sin pattern** that gives the enemy a legal right to operate in that area (Ephesians 4:26-27).

In this state, the individual is genuinely born-again and functional in many areas of their life. They love Jesus, read their Bible, and may even operate in spiritual gifts. Yet, they exhibit powerful compulsions, addictive behaviors, or chronic struggles in one specific area—be it lust, fear, a particular sickness, uncontrollable anger, or a spirit of poverty. They can relate to the Apostle Paul's agonizing description in Romans 7:15-23: **"For I do not understand my own actions. For I do not do what I want, but I do the very thing I hate... I see in my members another law waging war against the law of my**

mind and making me captive to the law of sin that dwells in my members." While Paul is describing the struggle with the indwelling sin nature, this "law" in his members can be, and often is, powerfully exploited and energized by an attached demonic spirit that amplifies the temptation and reinforces the bondage.

Third, there is Spiritual Attack.

This is fundamentally different from the first two, as it involves **external oppression, not an internal presence or attachment.** This is the enemy firing "fiery darts" (Ephesians 6:16) from outside the fortress of a believer's life. These attacks are often circumstantial and can be triggered by various factors:

- The **sins or curses of others** directed toward you (e.g., witchcraft, bitter words).
- **Stepping into a new level of destiny**, provoking a counter-assault from territorial spirits.
- **Strategic assignments** from demonic powers to hinder a specific work of God.

An attack may come through a difficult person who suddenly becomes a source of intense conflict (e.g., a hostile mother-in-law or a jealous colleague), a sudden and inexplicable reversal of fortune, or a overwhelming wave of accusation, fear, or discouragement that seems to come out of nowhere. The key diagnostic is that the spirit is *assailing* the person from the outside; it is not *inhabiting* or *attached* to them. A perfect biblical example is when Jesus turned to Peter and said, **"Get behind me, Satan!"** (Matthew 16:23). Jesus was not casting a demon out of Peter; He was recognizing and rebuking a satanic *attack* that was using Peter's well-intentioned but fleshly words as a vehicle. Peter was not possessed or demonized; he was under a strategic, external influence aimed at diverting Jesus from the Cross.

13.2 The Role of the Covenanted Deliverer

In an age that champions radical individualism and personal spiritual autonomy, the biblical model for deliverance presents a stark and necessary corrective. Deliverance is not a self-help technique, nor is it a solitary pursuit to be undertaken with only a Bible and personal resolve. While it is gloriously true that every believer has been given authority over all the power of the enemy (Luke 10:19), there are critical situations in spiritual warfare where the specific, corporate anointing and delegated authority of a **"covenanted deliverer"**—a God-appointed man or woman of God—are not just beneficial, but biblically mandated for breakthrough.

The Scripture provides clear precedent for this. James 5:14 instructs, **"Is anyone among you sick? Let him call for the elders of the church, and let them pray over him, anointing him with oil in the name of the Lord."** The prescription for a condition that may have spiritual roots is not merely personal prayer, but the invocation of covenantal authority through the recognized leadership of the local body. Furthermore, in a profound moment of spiritual disclosure, Jesus told Peter, **"Simon, Simon, behold, Satan demanded to have you, that he might sift you like wheat, but I have prayed for you, that your faith may not fail."** (Luke 22:31-32). Here, we see the principle of **representative intercession and authority**. Jesus, the ultimate Covenanted Deliverer, prayed for Peter, and that prayer formed a spiritual bulwark against a direct, satanic assault aimed at destroying Peter's faith and destiny. Peter, in that vulnerable moment, could not muster the spiritual fortitude on his own; he needed the covering of a higher, covenanted authority.

A God-appointed minister, specifically anointed for the ministry of deliverance, can operate in a dimension of authority and strategic insight that the individual under severe attack or entrenched attachment may not be able to access in their beleaguered state. This is not a matter of superior spirituality, but of divine assignment and the principle of spiritual covering. Such a deliverer functions in several critical capacities:

First, they can Pray Strategically. An individual may be fighting the symptoms—the spirit of lust, the fear, the sickness—while the deliverer, operating in a gift of discerning of spirits (1 Corinthians 12:10), can identify and directly assault the **"strong man"** (Matthew 12:29) that is overseeing the entire generational curse. They can trace the spirit back to its point of entry in the bloodline, bind the ruling principality, and plunder its house, freeing the individual from a systemic stronghold they may not even have been aware of.

Second, they Provide Spiritual Covering. The anointing resting upon a God-ordained minister creates a protective sphere of authority. When they engage in prayer and command, they are not operating as a private individual, but as a representative of Christ and His Church. This corporate authority can frustrate the enemy's attacks in a way that personal authority, especially when faith is wavering, sometimes cannot. It is the difference between a lone soldier facing an enemy platoon and that same soldier fighting under the covering air support of the entire air force.

Third, they Impart Truth and Faith. Often, individuals in bondage have had their minds so clouded by the enemy's lies that they cannot grasp the truths of their freedom. A covenanted deliverer, through teaching and prophetic declaration, can break through the mental strongholds and **awaken the individual to their rights in Christ.** They can rebuild the shattered foundations of identity, enabling the person not only to get free but to stand and maintain their freedom (Galatians 5:1).

This is precisely why it is spiritually dangerous to follow a leader or be part of a movement where the leader acknowledges no authority over themselves and creates no meaningful spiritual covering for those they lead. Such a model is alien to the New Testament, which is replete with the language of apostles, prophets, elders, and submission (e.g., 1 Corinthians 16:15-16, Hebrews 13:17). Deliverance is a function of the Body of Christ, a corporate endeavor where the strength of one member covers the weakness of another (1 Corinthians 12:21-26). To attempt to wage this level of warfare consistently in isolation is to ignore God's design and to invite unnecessary casualties. The covenanted deliverer is not a savior—that role belongs to Christ alone—but they are a God-appointed officer in the Lord's army, essential for leading certain difficult campaigns to victory.

13.3 Addressing the Attack

When a believer finds themselves under a sustained spiritual attack—a barrage of external circumstances, oppressive thoughts, or human opposition orchestrated by the enemy—the required response is fundamentally different from ministering deliverance for a spirit of attachment. The strategy here is not primarily expulsion or exorcism, for the enemy is not internally located. Rather, the biblical mandate is to engage in proactive **spiritual warfare and strategic advancement.** This is not a defensive crouch, but an offensive campaign waged from the unassailable high ground of our position in Christ. The goal transcends merely stopping the assault; it is to turn the enemy's attack into a divinely orchestrated opportunity for territorial gain, silencing the accusatory voices and reclaiming ground for the Kingdom of God.

The master blueprint for this conflict is detailed in Ephesians 6:10-18. The Apostle Paul leaves no ambiguity about the nature of the conflict: **"For we do not wrestle against flesh and blood, but against the rulers, against the authorities, against the cosmic powers over this present darkness, against the spiritual forces of evil in the heavenly places."** (Ephesians 6:12). This is a foundational hermeneutic for addressing attack. When the attack comes through a person—a hostile family member, a slandering coworker, a manipulative authority figure—the believer must, with spiritual discipline, look past the "flesh and blood" individual and discern the "principalities and powers" operating behind them. To wage war against the person is to fight on the enemy's chosen terrain of flesh and carnality, ensuring a futile and sinful conflict. The real battle is in the heavenlies, against the spiritual intelligence directing the human pawn.

The Apostle then outlines the full armor of God, which provides the comprehensive strategy for this warfare. This armor is not a collection of mystical charms but a representation of spiritual realities in Christ that we must consciously "put on."

- **The Belt of Truth (v. 14):** This is the first line of defense. In the face of an attack, often laden with deception, accusation, and confusion, the believer must actively gird themselves with the non-negotiable, objective truth of God's Word. This involves rejecting the enemy's narrative about your identity, your destiny, and your situation, and clinging to what God has declared. Every fiery dart of a lie must be met with the solid shield of "It is written..."

- **The Breastplate of Righteousness (v. 14):** An attack often includes accusations of unworthiness and past failure. The breastplate is the conscious standing in your gift of righteousness in Christ (2 Corinthians 5:21). You declare, "I am not fighting based on my own perfection, but on the perfect righteousness of Jesus Christ imputed to me. Your accusations have no legal standing." This protects your heart—the seat of your affections and conscience—from condemnation.
- **The Readiness of the Gospel of Peace (v. 15):** Even in the midst of conflict, your stance is one of unshakable peace because you are reconciled to God. This peace is not the absence of conflict but the presence of a covenant certainty that allows you to stand firm without being driven by anxiety or fear. Your feet are anchored in the good news that you are at peace with God, therefore no weapon formed against you can ultimately prosper (Isaiah 54:17).
- **The Shield of Faith (v. 16):** This is the active, moment-by-month trust in the promises and character of God. Faith "quenches all the flaming darts of the evil one." When the attack brings fear of financial ruin, faith declares God's provision. When it brings fear of failure, faith asserts God's predestined purpose. The shield is not passive; it is constantly moved to intercept each specific lie with a specific truth.
- **The Helmet of Salvation (v. 17):** This protects the mind. The attack is often aimed at your thought life, bringing doubt, confusion, and hopelessness. The helmet

is the assured hope of your complete salvation—past, present, and future. You actively guard your mind with the truth that your destiny is secure in Christ, and this present struggle is temporary.

Then, Paul reveals the **offensive weapons** that allow you to advance, not just defend:

- **The Sword of the Spirit, which is the Word of God (v. 17):** This is not merely owning a Bible, but the rhema—the spoken, timely, specific utterance of Scripture wielded in the Spirit against the enemy's tactics. Just as Jesus countered Satan's temptations in the wilderness with "It is written" (Matthew 4:1-11), you actively command the attacking spirits to retreat, you declare God's purpose over your situation, and you cut down strongholds of thought with the sharp, living truth of Scripture.
- **Praying at all times in the Spirit (v. 18):** This is the atmosphere in which the entire battle is fought. It is persistent, strategic, Spirit-led prayer. This includes praying in tongues, which builds you up and allows you to pray perfect prayers beyond your understanding (Jude 1:20), as well as intercession that specifically targets the spiritual forces behind the attack. This prayer is not a last resort; it is the continuous communication and coordination with the Commander-in-Chief, God Himself.

Therefore, addressing an attack is an active, aggressive, and strategic campaign. You are not a passive victim waiting for relief. You are a soldier, fully armored, advancing against the enemy's territory. You use the Word to silence the voices speaking against your destiny. You use prayer to bind the principalities orchestrating the conflict. You stand in your identity, and from that position of strength, you push back the darkness, not only securing your own freedom but establishing a beachhead of God's kingdom in the very area the enemy sought to destroy. The attack becomes the catalyst for your promotion and the enemy's defeat.

CHAPTER 14

The Sealing Power of Communion

Beloved, we approach now one of the most sacred and potent means of grace available to the believer in the ongoing work of securing freedom from generational strongholds. The Holy Communion, the Eucharist, the Lord's Supper—far from being a mere symbolic memorial or a religious tradition—is a dynamic, present-tense **covenant enactment.** For the warrior who has engaged in the spiritual warfare of breaking curses, Communion serves as the divine seal upon that victory, the continual application of the New Covenant's benefits to spirit, soul, and body, and a powerful proclamation that reinforces our separation from the old Adamic line.

14.1 Communion as a Covenant Meal

To comprehend the true power of the Lord's Table, we must first understand its original context within the framework of **covenant relationships**, which was the fundamental social and spiritual structure of the ancient Near Eastern world. A covenant was more than a contract; it was a sacred, binding bond that created a new, familial relationship between two parties, complete with promises, stipulations, and consequences. And a central, non-negotiable component of ratifying a covenant was the sharing of a **covenant meal.**

When parties entered into a covenant, they would slaughter an animal, divide it, and pass between the pieces (as seen in Genesis 15), signifying a self-maledictory oath: "May what has happened to this animal happen to me if I break this covenant." Following this solemn oath, the covenanting parties would then sit down together and share a meal. This meal was not merely a celebration. It was a participatory act of profound significance. To eat from the same bread and drink from the same cup was to symbolically internalize the very life and terms of the covenant. It was a tangible declaration: "The covenant is now in effect. Its blessings and obligations are entering into me and becoming part of my very being. We are now one."

It is within this rich, culturally understood framework that we must hear the words of our Lord Jesus on the night of His betrayal. Taking the cup, He said, **"This cup that is poured out for you is the new covenant in my blood."** (Luke 22:20, ESV). With this declaration, Jesus was instituting far more than a memorial service. He was establishing the participatory ratification meal of the **New Covenant**—the covenant foretold by Jeremiah, which would be unlike the old covenant written on stone, but one written on the heart, providing forgiveness of sins and an intimate knowledge of God (Jeremiah 31:31-34).

The broken bread represents His body, broken for us. The cup represents His blood, the blood of the covenant, poured out for the forgiveness of sins (Matthew 26:26-28). When we partake of the elements, we are not simply remembering a historical event. We are actively and spiritually **participating in the reality of that covenant.** We are reaffirming our place within its terms. We are internalizing its provisions. We are declaring, "I am in covenant with God through the blood of Jesus Christ. The life of this covenant—its blessings, its protections, its identity—is becoming my sustenance and my reality."

This has direct and powerful implications for breaking generational curses. The Apostle Paul explicitly states that **"Christ redeemed us from the curse of the law by becoming a curse for us."** (Galatians 3:13, ESV). The "curse of the law" encompasses every generational curse, every sickness, every form of poverty and death that the law pronounced upon disobedience (Deuteronomy 28:15-68). Our deliverance from this curse is a central provision of the New Covenant.

Therefore, every time we take Communion in faith, we are actively reaffirming our deliverance from that curse. We are partaking of the very body and blood that absorbed and exhausted the curse on our behalf. We are internalizing the legal reality of our freedom. We are stamping the victory of Calvary over every area of our lives, saying, "The terms of my old, cursed existence under Adam are null and void. I am now under the New Covenant in Christ's blood, and its provision for me is blessing, life, and freedom." The Communion table is where we regularly re-anchor our identity, renew our covenant consciousness, and seal our separation from the old, cursed bloodline by partaking of the new, life-giving blood of the Lamb.

14.2 The Body (The Bread): Breaking the Patterns

As we lift the element of the bread, we are engaging in an act of profound spiritual reception and declaration that strikes at the very root of physical generational strongholds. When we partake, echoing the words of our Lord, **"This is my body,"** we are doing far more than remembering a historical event. We are, through a faith-filled, participatory act, ingesting a spiritual reality. We are receiving and appropriating the wholeness, the soundness, and the sinless perfection of Christ's incarnate humanity as our own inheritance. This is the divine exchange made tangible: His body for our bodies, His wholeness for our brokenness.

The prophetic foundation for this is unshakable. The prophet Isaiah, gazing down the corridor of time, declared of the suffering Messiah: **"But he was pierced for our transgressions; he was crushed for our iniquities; upon him was the chastisement that brought us peace, and with his wounds we are healed."** (Isaiah 53:5, ESV). The Hebrew word for "healed" here is *rapha*, meaning to be cured, made whole, mended. The Apostle Peter reaffirms this in his first epistle, stating plainly, **"He himself bore our sins in his body on the tree, that we might die to sin and live to righteousness. By his wounds you have been healed."** (1 Peter 2:24, ESV). The body of Jesus was not broken by the Roman lash and the crucifixion for its own sake; it was broken as the perfect, final sacrifice to absorb into itself every consequence of sin, including every form of sickness, weakness, and physical corruption that has ever plagued humanity.

In the specific context of generational curses, the act of partaking of the bread becomes a powerful, judicial decree against the patterns of infirmity and physical brokenness that have traveled down family lines. When you take the bread, you are declaring, in the court of heaven and against the kingdom of darkness:

- **"The pattern of [specific sickness, e.g., heart disease, diabetes, cancer] that has afflicted my bloodline for generations ends its legal claim over my body now. It was absorbed into the body of Jesus on the cross."**
- **"The weakness and genetic predisposition toward [specific condition] is now superseded by the wholeness and vitality of Christ's resurrected body, which I now receive by faith."**
- **"The curse of deformity, chronic pain, or premature death has no legal standing in this body, for this body is now a temple of the Holy Spirit, and it partakes of the life of the One who conquered death itself."**

You are not merely hoping for healing; you are enforcing the finished work of the Cross over your physical being. You are proclaiming that the perfect, curse-free life of Jesus becomes the spiritual and physical template for your existence. His body was never touched by the curse of Adam; it was conceived by the Holy Spirit, lived in perfect submission to the Father, and then offered up as the unblemished Lamb to become the curse for us. When you ingest the bread by faith, you are asserting that this reality of a curse-free physical existence becomes yours. You are saying, "I receive the wholeness and the vital, resurrection life of Christ's body into mine. The old, broken record of my family's physical history is silenced by the testimony of His perfect body, broken for me."

This is a spiritual transaction of immense significance. It is a moment of active renunciation of the old inheritance and a conscious reception of the new. As you chew and swallow the bread, visualize and believe that the very life and health of the risen Christ are coursing through your veins, strengthening your bones, renewing your cells, and establishing a new, divine pattern of wholeness in your physical frame. The bread is your tangible point of contact to release faith for the breaking of every generational pattern of sickness and to seal your body into the covenant of healing purchased by the stripes of Jesus.

14.3 The Blood (The Cup): Silencing the Old Witness

We now come to the climactic moment of the sacred meal, the element that holds the supreme power to dismantle the very architecture of generational bondage. The cup is the divine antidote to the core problem we have labored to expose. As we lift the cup to our lips, we are engaging in the most potent spiritual act available to the believer for confronting and conquering the ancient curse. This is not a symbolic sip; it is a spiritual transaction of monumental proportions. We are, by faith, applying the **"sprinkled blood that speaks a better word than the blood of Abel"** (Hebrews 12:24) directly to the ledger of our lineage.

When we drink from the cup, we are spiritually flooding the very core of our being—our spirit, our soul, and yes, even our physical blood—with the triumphant testimony of Jesus. The voice of the old, Adamic blood, which has cried out for vengeance, judgment, and retribution since the day Cain slew Abel, has been the prosecuting witness against our bloodline for millennia. Its cry has been: **"Guilty! Unworthy! Cursed! Deserving of sickness, poverty, and death!"** This is the testimony that has empowered familiar spirits, reinforced destructive patterns, and given legal ground to generational curses.

But as you drink the cup, you are enacting a spiritual reality. You are declaring, with every fiber of your faith:

- **"The voice of my ancestral blood, which cried 'vengeance' for the sins of my fathers, is now silenced by the blood that cries 'mercy' and 'forgiveness.'"**
- **"The voice that testified to 'sickness' and 'infirmity' is drowned out by the blood that testifies to 'healing' and 'wholeness' (1 Peter 2:24)."**
- **"The voice that declared 'poverty' and 'lack' is overwhelmed by the blood that proclaims the 'riches' of His grace (2 Corinthians 8:9)."**
- **"The voice that echoed 'sin' and 'shame' is obliterated by the blood that roars 'righteousness,' 'redemption,' and 'justification' (Romans 5:9)."**

You are making a judicial declaration that the only voice with any legal authority over your life and your bloodline is the voice of the blood of the Lamb. This voice, speaking from the mercy seat in heaven, does not list your failures or your father's iniquities. It speaks a single, all-encompassing, eternal word: **"Forgiven."** It does not demand payment; it proclaims, **"Paid in Full."**

This act of drinking is a conscious act of renunciation and reception. You are renouncing your connection to the old, cursed testimony and receiving your place in the new, blessed testimony. As the liquid passes your lips and enters your body, visualize it as a divine flood, a spiritual tsunami of cleansing power, coursing through you, scouring clean the spiritual record of your bloodline, and silencing every demonic echo that has haunted your family for generations. You are, in that moment, applying the supreme court's final ruling to every lower court that has ever issued a judgment against you.

The cup is your personal enforcement of the New Covenant. The blood of Jesus is the seal of this covenant, and as you drink, you are stamping that seal over every area of your life—your health, your finances, your relationships, your mind. You are declaring that the old witness is void, its power broken, its voice mute. From this moment forward, the only testimony that matters is the one that speaks from Zion, the city of the Living God, and it speaks only of your acceptance, your freedom, and your glorious inheritance in Christ Jesus.

14.4 A Proclamation of Healing and Renewal

The consistent, faith-filled participation in the Lord's Table transcends a mere memorial of a past event or even a judicial declaration in the present; it also functions as a profound point of contact for tangible, supernatural life and health to be imparted to the believer. There exists a legitimate and powerful faith perspective, rooted in Scripture and confirmed by testimony, that rightly views Holy Communion as a vehicle for **physical healing, cellular renewal, and the reversal of the degenerative patterns inherited from the Fall.** This is not to promote a superstitious view of the elements, but to recognize that in this covenant meal, we are partaking of the very life of the resurrected Christ, and that life has tangible, physical consequences.

The testimony of the 98-year-old woman from my own ministry, who experienced a palpable sense of rejuvenation every time she partook of Communion, is not an isolated anecdote. It is a modern-day witness to a biblical principle. She understood, by revelation, that as she received the bread and the cup, she was receiving the *zoe* life of God—the very same resurrection life that raised Jesus from the dead (Romans 8:11). This life is inherently incorruptible and vitalizing. It stands in direct opposition to the law of sin and death that has operated in our bodies since Adam, a law that manifests in the generational patterns of decay, sickness, and aging.

This understanding finds a powerful correlation in the apostolic prayer of Paul for the Thessalonians: **"Now may the God of peace himself sanctify you completely, and may your whole spirit and soul and body be kept blameless at the coming of our Lord Jesus Christ."** (1 Thessalonians 5:23, ESV). The word "completely" here is *holoteles*, meaning "through and through, perfectly, in every part." Paul's prayer encompasses the entire human trifecta: spirit, soul, and *body*. He envisions a state of wholeness and blamelessness that is not reserved solely for the afterlife but is a divine intention for our present existence. The Communion table is a primary means through which this prayer is operationalized. As we receive the body and blood of Christ, we are inviting the God of peace to sanctify, to make whole, our entire being—including our physical bodies, which are susceptible to the genetic weaknesses and inherited predispositions of our bloodline.

When we partake of the bread, we are not only remembering a broken body; we are receiving the substance of a resurrected, glorified, and immortal body. We are, by faith, introducing the very essence of immortality into our mortality. The Apostle John captures this glorious truth in his first epistle: **"Whoever feeds on my flesh and drinks my blood has eternal life, and I will raise him up on the last day."** (John 6:54). While the ultimate fulfillment is the resurrection at the last day, the "eternal life" (*zōēn aiōnion*) is a present-tense possession for the believer. This is the uncreated, timeless life of God Himself. As we consistently "feed" and "drink" at His table, this eternal life works as a leaven of immortality within our mortal frame, counteracting the curses of decay and disease.

Therefore, the Communion table becomes a divine clinic. It is the place where we come to receive treatment for the soul-sickness of sin and the body-sickness of the curse. We are partaking of the Great Physician's own prescription: Himself. Every time we eat the bread and drink the cup in faith, we are making a proclamation: **"The degenerative pattern of the Fall ends here. The curse of aging, sickness, and weakness is reversed in me. I receive the incorruptible, resurrection life of Jesus Christ into every cell of my body, and I declare that my mortal body is being vitalized, renewed, and sanctified by His immortal life."** This is the ultimate defiance against the generational curse. It is not merely resisting a specific disease, but actively receiving a life so powerful that it swallows up death in victory (1 Corinthians 15:54).

CHAPTER 15

A Life Unshackled: Walking in Sustained Freedom

Beloved, we have now navigated the deep waters of legal standing, spiritual warfare, and covenant enactment. We have driven the stake of Christ's victory into the heart of the generational curse. But hear me clearly: the moment of breakthrough, as powerful and necessary as it is, is not the finish line; it is the starting gate. **Freedom is not a one-time event but a sustained walk.** Breaking a generational curse is a decisive legal victory in the heavenlies, but translating that victory into the daily reality of an unshackled life requires ongoing vigilance, spiritual wisdom, and the deliberate cultivation of a transformed lifestyle. The enemy, though legally defeated, is a master of deception and will seek to convince you that nothing has changed, that the old patterns are your inevitable destiny. Your mission is to live as if the victory is true—because it is—until your entire being aligns with that glorious reality.

15.1 The Necessity of Renewing the Mind

The foundational battlefield for maintaining freedom is the human mind. It is crucial to understand that a generational curse never operated by sheer spiritual force alone; it always worked in collusion with the soul—specifically, the **mind, will, and emotions.** The curse provided the legal ground, but the soul provided the welcoming environment, the familiar "rut" of thought and belief. For decades, even centuries, your family line has been conditioned to think in certain ways: "This is just how we are," "We're always sick," "Money never stays in our family," "Our marriages never work." These are not neutral observations; they are demonically inspired strongholds—fortresses of thought that have been built brick by brick through generations of negative experience and agreement with the curse.

Even after the spiritual legalities of the curse have been shattered by the blood of Jesus, the soul may remain trapped in this deeply grooved rut. The neural pathways of unbelief and defeat are well-worn superhighways in the brain. The emotions are conditioned to respond to triggers with fear, anger, or despair. The will is accustomed to yielding to certain temptations. This is why the Apostle Paul's command in Romans 12:2 is not a gentle suggestion but a non-negotiable mandate for sustained freedom: **"Do not be conformed to this world, but be transformed by the renewal of your mind, that by testing you may discern what is the will of God, what is good and acceptable and perfect."**

The Greek word for "transformed" is *metamorphoō*, from which we get "metamorphosis." It signifies a complete, fundamental change of form, like a caterpillar becoming a butterfly. This is God's goal for your thought life. But note the mechanism: this transformation happens "*by the renewal of your mind.*" This is not a passive, zap-from-heaven experience for which we simply wait. It is an active, deliberate, and sustained process of deprogramming and reprogramming.

The believer who would walk in sustained freedom must become a ruthless spiritual surgeon in the operating theater of their own mind. This involves:

1. **Systematic Demolition of Strongholds:** You must actively, using the weapon of divine truth, tear down every argument and lofty opinion raised against the knowledge of God (2 Corinthians 10:4-5). When the thought comes, "You'll always struggle with debt," you must immediately counter it with the truth: "My God supplies all my need according to his riches in glory in Christ Jesus" (Philippians 4:19). You must take that thought captive, try it in the court of God's Word, and execute it as a lie.
2. **Consistent Meditation on Scripture:** You cannot fight lies with vacuum. You must flood your mind with the truth. This means more than reading a verse a day. It means *chewing* on Scripture. It means taking a truth about your identity in Christ—"I am the righteousness of God in Christ" (2 Corinthians 5:21)—and repeating it, studying it, praying over it, and visualizing its reality until it becomes more real to you than the old, condemning narrative.
3. **Immersive Exposure to Anointed Teaching:** Your mind will be renewed by what it continually hears. You must saturate your environment with sound, anointed teaching that reinforces your new creation identity and the finished work of the Cross. This

is how faith comes (Romans 10:17)—by continually hearing the Word of Christ.

4. **Deliberate Rejection of Old Patterns:** You must learn to recognize the "echo" of the defeated curse. When a feeling of familiar despair, a wave of old fear, or a compulsive thought arises, you must not entertain it. You must not analyze it. You must recognize it as a ghost from a defeated kingdom and command it to leave in the name of Jesus. You reject its validity and instead affirm the truth of God's Word.

The renewed mind is the guardian of your freedom. It is the filter through which all circumstances must pass. It is the command center that interprets reality based on the victory of Zion, not the failures of the past. Without this renewal, the soul will continually drag the spirit back into the graveyard of the old curse, wondering why the legal victory doesn't "feel" real. But with a mind steadily renewed by the truth, you will walk in the manifest reality of your liberation, proving in your daily life what is the good, acceptable, and perfect will of God.

15.2 The Power of Proclamation

The awakened believer, having engaged in the renewal of the mind, must now master the primary weapon of enforcement in the spiritual realm: **the spoken word.** Your tongue is not merely an organ of flesh for tasting and communicating; it is a spiritual instrument of immense creative and destructive power. The entire created universe was summoned into existence by the spoken word of God (Genesis 1, Hebrews 11:3). You, being created in His image, have been endowed with a tongue that carries creative authority. To walk in sustained freedom from generational curses is to become proficient in using your tongue not to describe your prison, but to **enforce the victory of Christ** and decree the reality of your Zion citizenship into every sphere of your existence.

This spiritual discipline involves several distinct but interconnected practices:

First, there are Declarations of Identity. This is the foundational use of your tongue. You must daily, audibly, and with conviction affirm who God says you are in Christ. This is not positive affirmation; it is legal proclamation. The generational curse spoke a false identity over your bloodline for generations: "You are a slave, you are sick, you are poor, you are a failure." You must now overwrite that demonic recording with the truth of your new creation identity. You must declare, with your own voice:

- "I am a new creation in Christ Jesus; the old has gone, the new has come!" (2 Corinthians 5:17)
- "I am the righteousness of God in Christ Jesus." (2 Corinthians 5:21)
- "I am redeemed from the curse of the law." (Galatians 3:13)
- "I am more than a conqueror through Him who loved me." (Romans 8:37)
- "I am a chosen race, a royal priesthood, a holy nation, a people for God's own possession." (1 Peter 2:9)

These declarations are not for God's benefit; He already knows who you are. They are for your benefit, to train your soul to agree with your spirit, and they are for the enemy's benefit, to remind him of your legal standing. Every declaration is a hammer blow to the strongholds of the past, shattering the old, familiar lies and establishing the new, godly reality.

Second, there are Decrees of Breakthrough. While declarations affirm your state of being, decrees command your circumstances to align with that state. This is the aggressive, offensive use of your authority. Jesus said, **"Truly, I say to you, whoever says to this mountain, 'Be taken up and thrown into the sea,' and does not doubt in his heart, but believes that what he says will come to pass, it will be done for him."** (Mark 11:23). The "mountain" is any persistent, immovable obstacle that stands in opposition to God's will for your life—a mountain of debt, a mountain of sickness, a mountain of relational strife that has the fingerprints of a generational curse all over it.

You do not pray *about* the mountain; you speak *to* the mountain. You address it directly with the authority of Christ. You decree: "Mountain of debt, I command you to be removed and cast into the sea in the name of Jesus! I decree supernatural provision and financial breakthrough over my life." "Mountain of [specific sickness], I command you to be plucked up by the roots and cast out! I decree the healing power of Jesus to flow through my body." You are not begging God to do something; you are commanding the obstacle to move based on what He has already done. Your decree is the enforcement mechanism of Christ's victory in your specific situation.

Third, there is the Power of Thanksgiving and Praise. This may seem like a passive activity, but it is one of the most potent spiritual weapons. Thanksgiving and praise create a spiritual atmosphere. Demonic spirits, which thrive in an environment of complaint, fear, and despair, cannot operate in an atmosphere of heartfelt gratitude and joyful praise. When you give thanks to God for your freedom—even when you still feel the lingering echoes of the curse—and when you praise Him for His character and His victory, you are doing two things: you are fortifying your own faith, and you are constructing a divine habitation. The Psalmist declares that God is **"enthroned on the praises of Israel"** (Psalm 22:3). Your praise literally invites the manifest presence of the King of Kings into your situation. And in His presence, no curse can stand, no demon can remain, and every mountain must bow. Praise is the atmosphere of Zion, and as you fill your life with it, you make it an environment where your hard-won freedom can flourish and become permanent.

15.3 Guarding the Gates

The glorious freedom secured through legal victory, mental renewal, and authoritative proclamation is a territory that must be vigilantly guarded. To believe that once a curse is broken, one can return to the same environments, relationships, and habits that provided its foothold is a fatal error in spiritual strategy. The enemy, though his legal claim has been severed, is a strategic opportunist. He will constantly probe the defenses of your life, looking for an open gate through which he can attempt to re-infest and re-establish his former stronghold. Therefore, the believer must become a disciplined and discerning gatekeeper, for **freedom is not only attained through warfare; it is maintained through wisdom and watchfulness.**

The ancient wisdom of Proverbs 4:23 issues a perpetual command that is the cornerstone of sustained deliverance: **"Keep your heart with all vigilance, for from it flow the springs of life."** The Hebrew word for "keep" is *natsar*, meaning to guard, to watch, to preserve, to maintain a hedge around. The "heart" (*leb*) in Scripture represents the central core of a person—the mind, the will, the emotions, the inner life. This is the command center, and it is from this place that the course of one's life is determined. To guard it with "all vigilance" implies a conscious, active, and comprehensive defense strategy.

This defense is executed by controlling what enters the soul through its primary gates. King David, a man who understood both spiritual victory and tragic failure, declared his strategy: **"I will not set before my eyes anything that is worthless."** (Psalm 101:3, ESV). The "eyes" are one of the primary gates. What you choose to watch—the entertainment you consume, the images you linger on, the media you ingest—is not neutral. It is either reinforcing the new creation reality of Zion or it is subtly re-programming your soul with the values, fears, and lusts of the fallen world system, the very system that empowers generational curses.

But the gates are not only the eyes. The **ears** are another critical entry point. The voices you listen to—the cynical conversations, the ungodly counsel, the music with lyrics of despair and rebellion, the constant stream of bad news—all shape the atmosphere of your soul. The enemy specializes in using familiar voices from your past—a critical parent, a former partner, a toxic friend—to replay the old, cursed narrative in your mind. You must guard your ears, deliberately choosing to saturate them with the truth of God's Word, with anointed teaching, and with faith-filled fellowship.

Furthermore, you must guard the gate of your **associations and environments.** The people you allow into your inner circle and the places you frequent create a spiritual ecosystem. 1 Corinthians 15:33 warns, **"Do not be deceived: 'Bad company ruins good morals.'"** The Greek word for "company" is *homilia*, meaning companionship, intercourse, association. To return to relationships that were enmeshed with your old, cursed lifestyle—even with a heart to "witness" to them—is to stand on a spiritual landmine. To revisit environments where you formerly fell into sin or where the curse was most active is to invite a powerful spirit of remembrance and temptation. These places and people can carry a spiritual charge that acts as a trigger, attempting to reactivate the old, broken neural and spiritual pathways.

A lifestyle of **holiness** is not a set of restrictive rules; it is the strategic fortress that protects your hard-won freedom. Holiness (*hagiosmos*) means to be set apart, consecrated, dedicated to God's use. It is the conscious decision to build a life that is so distinctly aligned with the culture of Zion that the atmosphere of the old kingdom finds no point of entry. It is the practical outworking of being a "new creation." You are building a wall around the wellspring of your life, not to imprison yourself, but to protect the priceless water of freedom from being poisoned by the toxic runoff of the world. Every decision to turn away from a corrupting image, to leave a toxic conversation, to end a ungodly relationship, is another brick laid in the fortress wall. It is a declaration to your own soul and to the spirit realm: "This territory belongs to Jesus Christ, and the former occupant is not welcome to return." Your vigilance at the gates is the daily proof that you value your freedom more than you value the fleeting pleasures of Egypt.

15.4 Living as a Covenant Breaker and a Destiny Fulfiller

We have now reached the ultimate horizon of our journey, the profound and glorious purpose that transcends personal liberation and places your life within the eternal narrative of God's redemptive plan. The breaking of a generational curse is not an end in itself. It is not merely for your personal comfort, the alleviation of your suffering, or the achievement of your individual goals. These are blessed benefits, but they are not the ultimate objective. The supreme purpose is **the fulfillment of a divine destiny that has been held in suspension by the powers of darkness, a destiny that stretches beyond you to the generations yet unborn.** You are called to be the **"Abraham" of your lineage**—the covenant breaker to the curses of hell and the covenant establisher for the blessings of Heaven.

Consider the paradigm of Abraham. He stood in a lineage that was spiritually dead, in a "father's house" of idolatry. But his obedience to God's call to "go out" (Genesis 12:1) was not a self-serving act. It was a cosmic pivot point. He became the one who broke the chain of paganism and established a new covenant line with the Living God. His personal blessing—"I will bless you and make your name great" (v. 2)—was inseparably linked to a transgenerational purpose: "and in you all the families of the earth shall be blessed" (v. 3). His freedom was the gateway to a global redemption.

In the same way, your victory over the generational curses in your bloodline is a prophetic act with eternal ramifications. You are not just getting free; you are **cutting a new covenant channel** through the spiritual landscape of your family's history. The curses of darkness—of addiction, poverty, sickness, and strife—that flowed down one channel for generations are now, through your stand in Christ, dammed up, diverted, and rendered powerless. But you do not leave a void. You establish a new channel, dug by the truth of God's Word and cemented by the blood of Jesus, through which the blessings of God—of abundance, health, wisdom, and divine purpose—can now flow to your children, your grandchildren, and your great-grandchildren.

Your freedom and your subsequent success are not just for you. They are a **down payment**, a firstfruit, a tangible evidence of the blessing God always intended for your bloodline. When you walk in financial wisdom and break the curse of poverty, you are not just building wealth for yourself; you are establishing a new financial inheritance for your descendants. When you walk in marital fidelity and break the curse of divorce, you are not just enjoying a happy marriage; you are setting a new standard of covenant-keeping for your lineage. When you walk in divine health and break the curse of a specific disease, you are not just healing your body; you are creating a new genetic legacy of vitality. You are the living proof that the curse is broken, making it easier for those who follow you to step into their own God-given identity without having to fight the same foundational battles.

Therefore, you become a **covenant breaker** to the kingdom of darkness. You have legally and experientially shattered its claims over your family. And simultaneously, you become a **covenant establisher** for the Kingdom of God. You are the one who, like Joshua, stands between the generations and declares, **"But as for me and my house, we will serve the LORD."** (Joshua 24:15). You are planting trees of righteousness in a desert that was once your inheritance, knowing that the shade and fruit will bless those who come after you long after you are gone.

So, walk therefore. Do not walk in the lingering fear of the old curse, glancing over your shoulder as if the chains might somehow reattach themselves. Walk in the **conscious, joyful authority** of one who knows their legal standing. You are not a fugitive from darkness; you are an ambassador of light. You have been **"delivered... from the domain of darkness and transferred... to the kingdom of his beloved Son"** (Colossians 1:13). Your footsteps now fall on kingdom ground. Your voice now carries kingdom authority. Your life is now a kingdom outpost. The old bloodline's testimony is silenced. The new creation's destiny is activated. From this day forward, your life shall never be the same again, for you are no longer a victim of your past, but a pioneer of your future and a patriarch/matriarch of a new godly legacy.

APPENDIX

Prayers and Declarations for Breaking Bloodline Curses

A. Prayer of Renunciation and Repentance

Heavenly Father, Most Holy and Righteous Judge of all the earth, I approach Your throne of grace at this moment not in my own merit, but clothed in the majestic and all-sufficient name of Your Son, my Lord and Savior, Jesus Christ. I come in the full assurance of faith, standing upon the immutable truth of Your Word which declares that I am a chosen race, a royal priesthood, a holy nation, a people for Your own possession, that I may proclaim the excellencies of Him who called me out of darkness into His marvelous light (1 Peter 2:9). It is from this position of redemption and authority that I now undertake this solemn and critical spiritual transaction.

In the spirit of identificational repentance, as demonstrated by your servants Daniel (Daniel 9), Nehemiah (Nehemiah 1), and Ezra (Ezra 9), who humbled themselves and confessed not only their personal sins but the corporate iniquities of their fathers, I now come before You. By the illumination of Your Holy Spirit, and to the best of my knowledge, I acknowledge and bring into the searching light of Your presence the specific sins, transgressions, and iniquities of my forefathers, the generations that have preceded me in my paternal and maternal bloodlines.

Specifically, I bring before You the sins of [mention any known specific sins, for example: idolatry and the worship of false gods; all involvement with the occult, witchcraft, divination, spiritism, freemasonry, or secret societies; the sins of addiction to alcohol, substances, or perverted sexual pleasures; the sins of sexual immorality, adultery, fornication, pornography, and sexual abuse; the sins of violence, murder, hatred, and bloodshed; the sins of covenant-breaking, deceit, fraud, and thievery; the sins of bitterness, unforgiveness, and generational hatreds; the sins of pride, rebellion, and the rejection of Your divine authority; the sins of word curses, slander, and destructive speech spoken over this lineage].

I repent *on their behalf*. I stand in the gap as a priest of my bloodline, and I acknowledge the gravity of these transgressions against Your holy law. I also repent for any and every way that I, personally, have knowingly or unknowingly participated in, partnered with, or yielded to these same sinful patterns and spirits. I confess my own complicity and any ways I have given place to the devil (Ephesians 4:27) through my thoughts, words, or deeds.

Now, by the authority vested in me as a born-again believer and as an ambassador of the Lord Jesus Christ, I explicitly and vocally **renounce, revoke, and declare null and void** every single covenant, pact, vow, oath, or soul-tie that was ever made with darkness, with false gods, or with demonic powers by any member of my ancestral line. I renounce every dedication of children, every offering made to idols, every petition to familiar spirits, and every agreement with death and hell (Isaiah 28:15, 18) that was ever enacted by my forebears.

I declare that the legal power and binding authority of every one of these demonic covenants is forever shattered, broken, and dissolved by the supreme and all-powerful **blood of Jesus Christ.** Your Word declares that through death, Christ destroyed the one who has the power of death, that is, the devil (Hebrews 2:14). His blood is the blood of the New and Eternal Covenant, which speaks a better word than the blood of Abel (Hebrews 12:24). I apply that blood now, judicially, to the entire scroll of my generational history. I declare that every signature of hell on that document is now blotted out by the blood of the Lamb. The case is closed. The debt is paid. The curse is broken. From this moment forward, my lineage is under a new covenant, established on better promises, and I am a new creation in Christ Jesus. The old has passed away; behold, the new has come (2 Corinthians 5:17). In the mighty and victorious name of Jesus Christ, I pray. Amen.

B. Prayer to Break Curses

Almighty God, Eternal Father, I come before You now in the supreme, all-powerful, and victorious name of Your Son, the Lord Jesus Christ. It is in this name, the name that is above every name, that every knee must bow, in heaven and on earth and under the earth (Philippians 2:9-10). I approach the throne of grace with boldness and confidence, not based on my own righteousness, but as a blood-bought child, fully identified with Christ in His death, burial, and resurrection.

By the divine authority delegated to me as a believer and in full agreement with the legal victory accomplished at Calvary, I now take my stand against the kingdom of darkness. I address every principality, every power, every ruler of the darkness of this age, and every spiritual force of wickedness in the heavenly places that has presumed to have jurisdiction over my life and my lineage through generational curses.

In the name of Jesus, I now authoritatively **break, shatter, and loose** myself, my children, and my entire generational line from every generational curse, every demonic pattern, every cyclical stronghold, and every inherited assignment of hell. I specifically target and command to be broken:

- Every curse, pattern, and cycle of **[mention the specific area: e.g., poverty, financial lack, and debt]**.
- Every curse, pattern, and cycle of **[mention the specific area: e.g., sickness, infirmity, and specific diseases such as cancer, diabetes, or heart disease]**.
- Every curse, pattern, and cycle of **[mention the specific area: e.g., divorce, marital strife, and relational breakdown]**.
- Every curse, pattern, and cycle of **[mention the specific area: e.g., failure, stagnation, and inability to finish]**.
- Every curse, pattern, and cycle of **[mention the specific area: e.g., premature death, untimely demise, and ancestral mourning]**.

- Every curse, pattern, and cycle of **[mention the specific area: e.g., addiction, substance abuse, and slavery to sin]**.
- Every curse, pattern, and cycle of **[mention the specific area: e.g., mental illness, depression, anxiety, and mental oppression]**.
- Every curse, pattern, and cycle of **[mention the specific area: e.g., witchcraft, divination, and occult bondage]**.

I declare that the **blood of Jesus Christ, which speaks a better word than the blood of Abel**, has eternally silenced the voice of every one of these curses. The voice that cried "vengeance," "sickness," "poverty," and "death" from my ancestral line is now mute. It is overwhelmed, drowned out, and rendered null and void by the superior testimony of the Lamb's blood, which cries "mercy," "healing," "provision," and "life" from the true mercy seat in heaven.

I stand firmly upon the apostolic declaration of Galatians 3:13-14: **"Christ redeemed us from the curse of the law by becoming a curse for us—for it is written, 'Cursed is everyone who is hanged on a tree'— so that in Christ Jesus the blessing of Abraham might come to the Gentiles, so that we might receive the promised Spirit through faith."**

Therefore, I proclaim with absolute certainty: **I AM REDEEMED FROM THE CURSE OF THE LAW.** The legal basis for every curse—the broken law—has been satisfied in the body of Christ on the tree. The curse has no legal standing, no legal right, and no legal power over me or my descendants.

Consequently, I now walk consciously, deliberately, and perpetually under the **blessing of Abraham.** I receive the fulfillment of the promise that in Abraham's seed—who is Christ—I am blessed with every spiritual blessing in the heavenly places (Ephesians 1:3). The blessings of Deuteronomy 28:1-14 are my inheritance: I am blessed in the city and blessed in the country. I am blessed in my coming in and blessed in my going out. Everything I set my hand to prospers. I am the head and not the tail, above only and not beneath.

I declare that every generational pathway that once carried the toxin of the curse is now cleansed by the blood of Jesus and recalibrated to carry the blessing of the Lord. From this moment forward, my lineage is a conduit of divine favor, health, prosperity, and life. The cycle is broken. The pattern is severed. The curse is destroyed. I am free, my children are free, and my children's children are free, by the power in the name of Jesus and through His everlasting blood. Amen.

C. Declaration of Identity in Christ

I now rise in the full, conscious, and unwavering authority of my redeemed identity. I am not who my past says I am. I am not who my bloodline's history declares me to be. I am not the sum of my failures or the product of my ancestry. My identity is not found in the fallen lineage of Adam, but in the glorified person of Jesus Christ. Therefore, I lift my voice to make a proclamation that aligns my soul, my spirit, and my circumstances with the eternal, settled truth of God's Word.

I declare with absolute, unshakable faith: **I am a new creation in Christ Jesus.** This is not a future hope, nor a theoretical concept. According to the infallible authority of 2 Corinthians 5:17, this is my present-tense reality. The old, Adamic nature—with its predisposition to sin, its vulnerability to the curse, and its alignment with death—has been crucified with Christ and has passed away. It is rendered inoperative, a relic of a former kingdom. Behold, the new has come! I am a part of a new species of humanity, born from above, with a spiritual DNA sourced in the resurrection life of my Lord.

I affirm and enforce the reality of my position: **I am in Christ, seated in heavenly places in Him.** My physical location is temporal, but my spiritual citizenship and position are eternal. Ephesians 2:6 is not a metaphor; it is a legal fact. I am no longer operating from a position of earthly struggle, fighting *for* victory. I am seated in the place of supreme authority, far above all rule, authority, power, and dominion, fighting *from* the victory already secured by Christ (Ephesians 1:21). From this elevated position, I command the circumstances of my life to align with the triumph of Zion.

I proclaim my citizenship: **I am in Zion, the city of the living God, the heavenly Jerusalem (Hebrews 12:22).** I have come to this mountain by grace through faith. And in this Zion-reality, the prophetic decree of Isaiah 33:24 is my present-tense inheritance: **"No inhabitant will say, 'I am sick'; the people who dwell there will be forgiven their iniquity."** Therefore, I renounce and reject every symptom, every diagnosis, and every whisper of infirmity that contradicts the law of this kingdom. My body is a territory of Zion, and sickness is an illegal alien with no right to reside here. Furthermore, my iniquity—both personal and generational—has been forgiven, sent away, and remembered no more. The legal ground for any curse has been utterly annihilated by the blood of the covenant.

Based upon this unassailable foundation, I decree:

- **The generational patterns are broken.** The cycles of failure, the chains of addiction, the echoes of poverty, and the shadows of sickness end their reign now. They have no power to replicate themselves in my life.

- **I walk in divine health.** The resurrection life of Christ, which cannot be contained by sickness or death, is my vital source. His wholeness permeates my spirit, soul, and body.
- **I walk in prosperity.** I am a conduit of Heaven's economy. The blessing of Abraham is upon me, and I am empowered to create wealth and steward resources for the advancement of God's Kingdom.
- **I walk in victory.** I am more than a conqueror through Him who loved me (Romans 8:37). Every battle is an opportunity to manifest a victory already won.

I make this supreme declaration of destiny: **What stopped my forefathers will not stop me.** The giants that defeated them are decapitated corpses at my feet. The limitations that defined them are shattered beneath my feet. The curses that hindered them are nullified by the blood over me.

I am a destiny fulfiller, to the glory of God. I am not an accident of history or a victim of heredity. I am a chosen instrument, fashioned for good works which God prepared beforehand so that I should walk in them (Ephesians 2:10). I will complete my assigned race. I will fulfill my God-given purpose. I will leave a legacy of blessing, establishing a new godly line for generations to come. All of this is for the everlasting glory of God the Father, through the power of God the Son, by the presence of God the Holy Spirit. Amen.

www.ingramcontent.com/pod-product-compliance
Lightning Source LLC
LaVergne TN
LVHW022044200926
848481LV00003B/781